Britain's Great Immigration Disaster

– GAVIN COOKE –

An environmentally friendly book printed and bound in England by
www.printondemand-worldwide.com

Mixed Sources
Product group from well-managed
forests, and other controlled sources
www.fsc.org Cert no. TT-COC-002641
© 1996 Forest Stewardship Council
FSC

PEFC Certified
This product is
from sustainably
managed forests
and controlled
sources
www.pefc.org
PEFC
PEFC/16-33-418

This book is made entirely of chain-of-custody materials

www.fast-print.net/store.php

Britain's Great Immigration Disaster
Copyright © Gavin Cooke 2012

ISBN 978-178035-310-4

First published 2012 by
FASTPRINT PUBLISHING
Peterborough, England.

Contents

Gavin Cooke

Chapter fourteen: What Is To Be Done?

Glossary/Bibliography

Introduction

On October 20, 2010, like millions of others watching the news on television, I heard the Coalition Chancellor George Osborne announce a range of drastic austerity measures. Major cuts in the cost of our social welfare system needed to help reduce a huge national deficit that was close to bankrupting Britain.

So we could avoid the fate of already bankrupt Greece and Ireland there would be budget cuts totalling £83 billion that would result in almost half a million jobs lost in the public sector. Yet in all the news bulletins and analysis on BBC and ITV news that day not once was the cost of immigration mentioned as part of this fiscal equation. I was left to reflect that not even Stalin, gripped by the madness of soviet doublethink, could have contrived a more complete control of the political agenda.

Since 1997 Britain has seen the biggest population change in its long history, changes overseen and approved by the New Labour administrations of Tony Blair and Gordon Brown.

There was never any vote on the matter and there hasn't been a parliamentary debate on immigration within living memory, despite the arrival on British soil of more than five million foreign nationals over the period 1997 to 2010.

Yet such is the panic over the levels of public debt needed to subsidise this unprecedented influx running through every government department in Whitehall that Coalition Prime Minister David Cameron felt compelled to break ranks and acknowledge the crisis. His speech on immigration in Southampton on April 10, 2011 where he talked of reversing the trends of the last 13 years and reducing annual net migration to "tens of thousands rather than hundreds of thousands by 2015" has no chance whatsoever of being translated into effective action as huge numbers of immigrants continue to arrive on our shores.

There has been virtually no removal and deportation of failed asylum seekers and illegal entrants to Britain before or since Cameron's speech. In the months between July and September 2011 removals and voluntary departures fell by 13% compared to the same period in 2010, with less foreign national prisoners sent home. Asylum applications also continued to rise in 2011, to 4,912, the highest level for two years with increasing numbers of asylum claims coming from Pakistan, Iran, Somalia, Syria and sub-Saharan Africa.

Cameron knows that the negative effects of mass immigration cannot be reversed without resort to draconian measures which no liberal democratic government could ever contemplate.

What he also knows is that up to a million of the 3.2 million new citizens and their families welcomed to Britain since 1997 will remain permanently unemployed and dependent on welfare benefits from an ever shrinking welfare cake.

The New Labour opposition that created this disaster in government and the Liberal Democrats, (now sharing power with the Conservative Party) never had the proverbial cigarette paper's difference between them over immigration policy.

Such is the stranglehold of political correctness now backed by the full force of the law that the politicians who run the Westminster club cannot bring themselves to even debate the measures needed to control immigration in case they are accused of racism. This prism of political correctness through which New Labour looked at the world and which allowed such enormous numbers of people unrestricted access to Britain's welfare state is still in place.

Though mass immigration was not the initial cause of Britain's current fiscal crisis it will seal Britain's financial collapse within the next 10 years as we try to cope with an expanded population at a time when millions of native Britons, resident here before 1997, will remain without work.

Mass immigration will ensure the end of the NHS, social security, pensions and the complete transformation of British society. The Conservatives, as part of a coalition government with the Lib-Dems, can't even point to the elephant that's now bigger than the room itself without risking a split that will see them lose power.

According to the Office for National Statistics (ONS), almost every new vacancy created by the economy run by New Labour since 1997 went to a foreigner. Immigrants filled 98.5 % of the 1.67million new jobs generated under 13 years of New Labour rule.

There is no other country in the world that has ever allowed its economy to be distorted on such a scale by the importation of workers from overseas.

The fractional benefit to the UK economy brought by these workers will prove to be an irrelevance when compared to the huge financial burden their permanent residence places on Britain.

The Labour Party was founded at the beginning of the 20th century to represent the interests of the British working-class yet the consequences of New Labour's betrayal of Britain's working class in favour of foreign labour will leave a bitter legacy of poverty and despair over generations. No work, no decent education or pensions and no health service of any note left for families whose parents and grandparents sacrificed much to provide the building blocks of a free and civilised society, the envy of the world.

Based on statistics provided by the ONS we now know that 5.2 million immigrants were allowed to settle in Britain during New Labour's tenure in office. Before New Labour came to power net immigration to Britain was about 40,000... that's 40,000 in a whole year, bear that figure in mind.

"These late eclipses in the sun and moon portend no good to us." **- King Lear**

Chapter One
Space Not Race.

Between 1997 and 2010 more than 5.2 million foreign nationals came to live in Britain. When we take into account the number of mostly white indigenous Britons who subsequently moved abroad after 1997 it left the net foreign-born population of the UK 3.2 million higher in 2010 than it was when New Labour first came to power in 1997 and of these 3.2 million new immigrants more than 80% came from countries outside the EU.

One in five of the population in Britain is now foreign born and this will rapidly increase as the baby boom currently taking place among new immigrant mothers kicks in.

That 3.2 million figure alone is equivalent to three times the population of the UK's second largest city, Birmingham and by 2031 will have increased to the equivalent of eight times the population of Birmingham, because of an accelerating immigrant birth rate. Where are they all to live?

Jonathan Porritt, a patron of the Optimum Population Trust (OPT) and former adviser to Gordon Brown on green issues has advocated that the population of Britain needs to be reduced from its current level of 62 million to 30 million if we are to be able to live in a sustainable society. That's less people than there were around when Queen Victoria was on the throne.

Instead, because of immigration, the number of people living in the UK will be more than 70 million and climbing in less than 15 years from now.

If we started building one new house every six minutes right now, just to cater for this population increase, we would still be building in 20 years time. Again, the official figure for immigration does not take into account the one million illegal immigrants who entered the country over the same period of time.

Some forecasters say one million is a gross underestimate and the figure is nearer two million but even at one million it means that one new immigrant per minute came to stay in Britain during the 13 years New Labour was in power. By 2031 will we see swathes of concrete paving over England's green fields and hedgerows?

There is no doubt that the transformation of Britain's landscape is already underway. The Coalition government's new presumption in favour of building development is indication enough that the English countryside will need to make way for housing. There are thousands of families now living in London whose housing benefit payments are to be reduced to £400 a week maximum, a policy of the Coalition government.

People like the family of Saeed Khaalif who live in a six bedroom house in West Hampstead with a rental value of

£4,300 a week. Khaalif has not worked since he arrived in Britain three years ago from Somalia yet he continues to reside in a property worth in excess of £2million. Housing benefit currently costs the taxpayer in excess of £20 billion a year. How much of this massive total subsidises migrants arrived in the UK since 1997? It is not unreasonable that these facts are revealed to the public who subsidise these families. Cases like that of the Khaalif's illustrate the utter pointlessness of surveys that look at the contribution made to the economy by migrants without taking their "welfare baggage" into account.

It won't be mentioned by the contractors paid to rip out the heart of the nation's green spaces because it's still a politically correct secret that a large percentage of new suburban housing sprawl will be filled by those immigrants currently living in London whose housing benefits are soon to be reduced to £400 a week maximum.

Those who can no longer afford to live where the rents exceed £400 a week will be encouraged to move, most likely northward where for £1600 a month a four or five bedroom house is easily within reach of families promised a life away from the now unaffordable London metropolis. The burden of extra payments needed for welfare baggage like education and health will fall on local councils who will find themselves very quickly running out of funds and closing libraries and old peoples' homes to compensate.

In 2008, research from a cross-party parliamentary group on immigration co-chaired by former Labour minister Frank Field showed that the population of the UK would reach 70 million by 2028 unless immigration falls by 190,000 a year between now and then. There is no chance of that ever happening, despite the best intentions of Mr Cameron, because immigration in 2011 is rising faster than ever. Frank Field is clearly worried about the future in the light of current Coalition policy. In 2011 the latest immigration data from the independent Office for National Statistics (ONS) estimated that the British population will rise from 61.8 million to more than 70 million in 2026, two years earlier than Field's group forecast in 2008 and that 68?% of the rise will be due to the effects of immigration.

The need for enough new housing to create seven cities the size of Birmingham predicted by Field has now become eight new cities the size of Birmingham.

There are currently more than three million people on council waiting lists for social housing. Field says that in order to house the immigrants waiting for somewhere to live now, not those still entering the country, more than 200 homes will need to be built every day, for 23 years. New Labour were well aware of this crisis before 2010 when John Prescott's Communities Plan proposed building 556,000 homes on 44 square miles of green field land creating four growth areas: Milton Keynes, Stansted in Essex, Ashford in Kent and the Thames Gateway.

The Thames Gateway development was to see 200,000 new homes being built in a 40-mile development from inner London to Southend and Medway by 2015 with the number of houses then built doubling to 400,000 by 2030. Green campaigners believe that there are more than 166 square miles of green belt already earmarked for development. The Coalition know the extent of this need to concrete over rural Britain and rather than calling a halt have taken up New Labour's cudgels by changing the planning laws to make it easier for developers to get building permission. Thus 3,000 acres of green belt will be paved over every year, say campaigners, with large building companies like Taylor Wimpey having a guaranteed market for their homes among the thousands of families moving out of London because of the £400 a week benefit cap. These homes are needed to house immigrant families and create desperately needed jobs, so why not admit it?

The bigger question is what happens when these new arrivals are ensconced in their shiny new homes and the building boom is over. New work in the building sector without the support of an expanding manufacturing base and a continuously growing economy will only provide a short term fix for the jobless. How long will it be before these housing estates become ghettos filled with feral youth and gang crime exported from the capital?

It's worth repeating, between 2002 and 2010 net non-EU immigration to Britain, that's mostly Africans and Asians who came to stay permanently in Britain, was more than 200,000 a year. In 2010 this figure had jumped to 239,000. These figures take no account of illegal immigration and so are an official underestimation. Officially, no one knows exactly how many illegal immigrants there are in the UK. New Labour allowed this foreign invasion to take place, but for what possible reason?

The answers most frequently trotted out by ministers were that immigrants were needed to fix a chronic labour shortage in Britain and so promote growth; that diversity was good for the nation and that lazy Brits wouldn't work so we needed a new imported workforce.

Yet even a cursory glance at the figures will show that economic expansion was already taking place in Britain before New Labour decided to throw UK borders wide open after their 1997 election win.

It doesn't take a genius to know that in the short term immigration will bring economic growth to any nation

11

because the more people there are the more economic output there is. However, economic growth in itself is of no value to the nation's wealth as a whole unless it brings with it increased output per head. You can have more economic "growth" because of more immigrants making more stuff for business to sell abroad, but that won't make the average citizen any better off unless there's a rise in general productivity.

No matter how many people you have in the country if you can't get them to produce more per head then the average person is no better off. If this can't be achieved by negotiation or new technology then a short term fix is to bring in immigrant labour. What New Labour did was create a short term solution to productivity decline but excluded from its calculations was the blindingly obvious; that immigrants themselves create the need for more services. Also never considered was that without increased productivity the only logical way to meet the new demands generated from immigration was by…. more immigration.

The big New Labour lie about immigration was to take the output of new immigrants and divide it by the UK's total output calling the resulting fractional growth "the economic benefit of immigration to the UK" .

Controlled immigration restricted to those with specific skills is a benefit to any advanced economy, helping industry to increase productivity per head. Mass immigration brings no benefits at all, only increases in productivity can make us all any better off.

The government report in January 2012 claiming that immigrants make up 8% of the population and contribute 10% to GDP was immediately found wanting by MigrationWatchUK who provided evidence that immigrants actually make up 10% of the population but contribute 9.8% to GDP, making them a net drag on the economy. There will be many more reports like this arguing for and against the value of mass migration to the economy. What such reports studiously ignore is that migrants now living here permanently and their future dependants will add huge numbers to the population and that will add massively to the future costs of the NHS, social services and pensions.

Any report claiming a fractional increase in GDP per head of immigration is just another political diversion if it does not acknowledge, then itemise these additional future costs. That's what we really need to know. What effect will mass immigration have on Britain on a step by step basis?

Beginning with the permanent changes; it will destroy large swathes of the countryside as new dwellings need to be built to house new arrivals and an expanding population; the culture as this expanding population, without assimilation, absorbs none of the values and norms necessary for integration into a modern democratic state; without continuous economic growth this expanded population bankrupts the country because if the new arrivals are not working they will need to rely on welfare benefits, social housing and the NHS.

The education bill alone will be colossal. The ONS estimate that up to the year 2020 Britain will need to fund an extra one million school places because of births in the UK to foreign born parents. In 2012 more than 84% of births in the London borough of Newham are to at least one foreign born parent. Based on costs per pupil in 2009, the cost of these additional school places will be almost £100 billion over ten years, that's nearly £10 billion a year. The only possible justification for spending on this scale is if the tax contribution to the economy of these migrants outweighs the tax burden of the increased costs they place on the education system. It does not, not by a long chalk.

What must be regarded as the greatest scandal since Watergate is that the total cost of the economic burden lumped on the British taxpayer by an unprecedented and unasked for influx of foreigners is still not in the public domain. Is this information being concealed by politicians who fear a backlash such statistics could provoke among outraged voters?

Neither New Labour or the Coalition are willing to separate or itemise the "cost of immigration" figures from the more generalised budgets dealing with the NHS, education, justice system, social security etc. The British public were never consulted over the decisions made to allow such a massive change and this makes it essential that they are now privy to how their money is still being spent. Without these figures the whole nature of democratic legitimacy in Britain must be called into question because a large majority of the electorate now have the uneasy feeling that in Britain anything goes on the say so of those in power. That's the same uneasy feeling George Orwell warned us about.

We can take a closer look at New Labour's argument for immigration by examining the rate of unemployment in any given year when immigration was at its peak. Let's take a year at random, a year when over 567,000 new arrivals were allowed to settle in Britain permanently....2007.

In 2007 Britain's jobless total was rising twice as fast as the European average, between December 2007 and October 2008 Britain had the third sharpest increase in unemployment, behind Spain and Ireland. Over the same period unemployment in France went up by just 0.1 per cent and in Germany it fell 0.8 per cent. Surely we weren't short of workers looking for jobs in 2007?

No we were not, because at the beginning of 2007 unemployment in the UK already totalled more than 1.92 million (with 27,000 jobs being lost at Woolworths alone), a jobless rate of 6.1%. Yet while unemployment steadily climbed from 2007 onwards so did the number of immigrants allowed to settle in Britain. Were all of the nearly two million British jobseekers that year so lazy that 567,000 more foreigners were needed to settle in Britain permanently to compete with them?

This unlikely scenario was New Labour's argument but its logic may well have escaped all those signing on. Following the introduction of the Nationality, Immigration and Asylum Act in 2002 by Tony Blair's government the number of foreigners arriving in Britain to live skyrocketed to more than half a million every year, and continues to this day despite the continuing level of British joblessness. These are the official figures, arrivals in bold. 2003: **512,000** 2004: **582,000** 2005: **565,000** 2006: **591,000** 2007: **567,000** 2008: **590,000** 2009: **567,000** 2010: **591,000**

Net immigration in 2010 increased by 21% with 239,000 more people arriving in the UK than were leaving. Most of those who were going for good were native British, born and bred. According to ONS statistics 336,000 native white British people left our island shores for good in 2010 while 575,000 immigrants came to Britain to settle permanently, most from outside of Europe.

Cameron's ludicrous rhetoric about reducing the flow of immigrants to tens of thousands shows just what kind of virtual world British politicians are living in.

If we removed not tens of thousands but hundreds of thousands, that's removal..... not just reducing the flow of new arrivals, it would still take more than a decade just to extract those who are here illegally. We would still be burdened with more than three million permanent new residents and their dependents who will contribute next to nothing to our economy over the coming decade because there will be no return to traditional cycles of economic growth, ever.

The ONS says that the population of England will increase by 10 million over the next 24 years, and 70% of this increase will be due to immigration. (1)

Their estimate is that the UK's population will increase by almost one per cent every year until 2020, that means half a million more people every year.

These are truly shocking figures. If we can't pay for our schools, hospitals and social care now what will happen over the next decade and beyond when these institutions have to cope with a million more customers every two years?

Over 300 languages are currently spoken in London schools, some of the most common are Punjabi, Bengali, Gujarati, Cantonese, Mandarin and Hokkien and in London there is an army of linguists on hand to translate 999 calls into any one of 150 different languages because nearly a third of all the people who live in London, over three million out of 8 million, don't speak English as their first language. How much of the money that we spend on translators in London alone could be used to pay for better emergency services or winter fuel payments for the elderly or grants for students?

Yet how do we know what was spent? We don't because under New Labour such information was a closely guarded secret. That information won't feature in any Panorama or Newsnight special because of the unofficial black-out of media coverage on the issue; immigration is not a subject the BBC wants discussed by the general public.

A former BBC producer Rod Liddle explained why the issue is taboo: "It is often said by its critics that the BBC has an inherently left wing bias across its output. I don't think this is correct. It is certainly biased, but it is not, to my mind, a left-wing bias: it is a metropolitan liberal bias... We are ruled by the ideas of London - or, to be more accurate, a certain arrogant and affluent part of it. A gilded crescent that stretches from Ealing in the west to Hoxton in the east, south to Dulwich, Greenwich and Wimbledon, and north to Hampstead Garden Suburb. From within this place emanate all the shibboleths of Politically Correct Britain, and its epic sense of rectitude that no person in public life dare challenge. Evangelistically secular, socially ultra-liberal and unwilling to allow even the mildest challenge to its political hegemony. And you can see why; for the London middle class, immigration, for example, means nicer food on the high street, cheaper nannies and plumbers and mini-cab drivers and so on. (But this is just the London middle class: to be sure, there are plenty of parts of London that should also be designated Not-London; the poorer nastier bits, where these views do not hold sway). Beyond London, out in the desolate wilds of Not-London, i.e. the rest of England, the economics do not work in quite the same way."(2)

This "gilded crescent" got a wake-up call when rioting broke out all over the capital in August 2011. Metropolitan Police statistics showed that of those arrested (and bearing in mind the hardcore largely evaded arrest) 55% were black or Asian and 13% were members of gangs. The number of foreign born members of the British population has almost doubled in the last 20 years to 10% with one in three Londoners being foreign born.

As relative calm returns to the streets of riot torn north London and even leafy Ealing the metropolitan liberal elite may breath a collective sigh of relief that it's all over now.

They couldn't be more wrong. The unvarnished truth is that the London riots of August 2011 will come to be seen as the beginning of a more generalised descent towards social disorder and criminality in England, with London at its epicentre.

What we have just witnessed is British multiculturalism being ripped apart at the seams by social upheaval brought on by more than a decade of mass immigration subsidised by the welfare state and the taxpayer.

Thanks to New Labour's reckless immigration experiment we must face the dystopian nightmare of an overpopulated nation plagued by energy shortages and growing unrest from resentful migrants, fearful trade unionists and a swelling underclass of criminals.

"Labour lied to people about the extent of immigration and the extent of illegal immigration and there's been a massive rupture of trust."

- Maurice Glasman.

Chapter Two
Hideously White

These are the words of Maurice Glasman, senior adviser to Labour leader Ed Miliband during New Labour's long period in office. He's now Baron Glasman, after being recommended for a peerage by Ed Miliband.

Safely ensconced in the Lords Baron Glasman now obviously feels free to say what he really believes. Writing in Labour's in-house magazine Glasman describes how New Labour was completely taken over by a politically correct elite who went to war with their traditional working class supporters. "Working class men can't really speak at Labour Party meetings about what causes them grief, concerns about their family, concerns about immigration, love of country, without being stereotyped as sexist, racist, nationalist," he said. (1)

In 2009 a leading London newspaper published an article by Andrew Neather, a government advisor who wrote speeches for Tony Blair, Jack Straw and David Blunkett. The article was about a policy document published by the Home Office, then headed by Jack Straw, in January 2001. The paper, Migration: An Economic and Social Analysis, was produced by a New Labour think-tank, the Performance and Innovation Unit. Its author was a civil servant Jonathan Portes, sometime speech writer for Gordon Brown and a senior aide to Cabinet Secretary Gus O'Donnell.

Neather claimed that in the drafts he read of this policy document there was an obvious political purpose to the new initiative: "that mass immigration was the way that the Government was going to make the UK truly multicultural". After discussions during the process of the paper's creation, Neather said that he had come away with a belief that what the New Labour leadership wanted was: "to rub the Right's nose in diversity and render their arguments out of date". (2)

After the policy document's initial Westminster circulation Neather wrote a ground-breaking speech in September 2000 for the then immigration minister Barbara Roche, calling for a loosening of what was left of Britain's immigration controls. The true scope and purpose of the new policy was to be kept secret from the electorate at large and from New Labour's core white working-class voters in particular, neither of whom were ever to have any say in this shift of policy allowing open-door immigration on a hitherto unheard of scale.

The paper turned out to be hugely influential and gave the green light to a second wave of mass immigration following the initial inflow that occurred hard on the heels of New Labour's election in 1997.

Thus the welcome mat was rolled out even wider after 2001 when 2.3 million more migrants were added to the population, with their dependants to follow. The consequences of these actions will come back to haunt us all but we need to remember that these policy proposals weren't in New Labour's election manifesto; there was no vote in cabinet, no debate in Parliament and no referendum allowed on this nation transforming policy.

From 1997 successive New Labour immigration ministers told us: "Britain has always been a nation of immigrants" but if the facts were never there to back up that claim and the historical evidence was always there to counter the rubric, if you cared to look it up. One of New Labour's biggest celebrity supporters Eddie Izzard focused on the question of English national identity in Mongrel Nation (2003) broadcast on Channel Five. Izzard's theory was that the English weren't really English at all but a product of foreign invasions and centuries of immigration. A stunning insight from a failed accountancy student.

Here's a brief journey into the recorded past clearly overlooked by Izzard's researchers. Between 1066 and 1945 Britain actually had very few waves of immigration. By far the largest were the Irish during the 19th century and technically they weren't immigrants since Ireland was part of the United Kingdom. Even these so-called immigrants never amounted to more than three per cent of the British population at the time then declined to about one per cent by the 1920s. (3)

The next largest group, the Jews, came to Britain from about 1880 to 1910 and their impact enriched Britain's intellectual, economic and cultural life; but how many came to Britain to live? Answer; about 150,000, then another 70,000 who fled the Nazis 40 years later. That's a total of around 220,000, period. That's about half the number of immigrants who entered the UK on any given year between 2007 and 2011. So much for New Labour's "nation of immigrants". Before 1997 all of the immigrant groups who ever reached our shores never amounted to more than one per cent of the total population. The Normans conquered, kicked us around, took our land and changed the fabric of our society, but they were a tiny, tiny elite.

None of these facts ever entered into the public domain because in 1997, with the election of New Labour, Britain was being ruled for the first time in its history by a government with a distinct ideology, political correctness (PC).

New Labour politicians used PC as a prism through which they filtered out the facts of life that didn't fit in with their spin. The fact that somewhere would have to be found for at least three million more people to live, a factual reality resulting from their policies, was never considered.

For New Labour there was an immediate enemy within and incredibly the target of its venom were those who were once its core supporters, the white working-class. People like traditional Labour voter Gillian Duffy, the 66-year-old widow Gordon Brown called " a bigoted women" because she dared to voice her fears over immigration from Eastern Europe during the 2010 General Election campaign.

Once thought of as the victims of the power elite, a phrase coined by Marxist thinker Ralph Miliband (yes... that's Labour leader Ed Miliband's dad), the working class were no longer the huddled masses once idolised by the left. They had voted in Margaret Thatcher three times and were never to be trusted again. What the left needed was a new class of huddled masses, one less likely to ever vote Tory again, so they set about importing one. This Trojan horse was to be mass immigration, New Labour's change agent.

That wave of immigrants are now adding one per cent to Britain's population every two years, and more than five per cent every decade. This is a fact largely unknown among the general public. That's a huge number, and these numbers have to be sought out and prised away from official sources with great difficulty.

At the time when New Labour let rip and allowed in anyone who wanted to come to Britain and stay without hindrance, after 2001, net migration swelled by more than 200,000 people every year. Bear in mind that does not include the tens of thousands who arrived illegally. Nor does it include the thousands of asylum seekers who were officially refused asylum but who decided to stay on in Britain anyway, were never deported and have since had full access to Britain's NHS and welfare benefits. As almost every illegal immigrant knows, once safe inside British borders there is virtually no chance of ever being removed.

If it had been suggested to the man in the street just 15 years ago that what used to be reasonably described as the white Christian majority population of Britain would become a minority in most major English cities by 2030 the reaction would have undoubtedly been astonishment followed by hilarity.

Today that suggestion would produce no such reaction. Britain has been invaded and colonised with the collaboration of New Labour and political correctness. All of us in Britain are about to watch the consequences of an experiment in political dogma unfold which will add seven million more people, mostly recent immigrants and their dependents, to Britain's already groaning population.

In New Labour's case the mantra of diversity was so pervasive that it allowed the rapid rise within their ranks of politicians who believed that the social structure of Britain had a toxic kite mark. New Labour politicians saw themselves as citizens of the world first and foremost and patriots a very poor second, if at all.

Never having had real jobs or much to do with people outside of their university-straight-to-politics career encouraged ambitious PC politicians, BBC opinion makers and members of the judiciary to label opposition to immigration as a form of racism, painfully evidenced by Gordon Brown's remarks in Rochdale during the 2010 election campaign.

Since 1999, more than 80% of Britain's annual increase in population has been because of immigration and the economic fallout from this has been scandalously hushed up.

What were supposed to be the benefits of multiculturalism? Diversity was the New Labour mantra but as it turned out what high culture arrived in tandem with the masses from Pakistan, Somalia, Nigeria or Bangladesh or the myriad other third world refugee's that were given open access to Britain to justify that claim?

What books or music that could not be accessed over the internet, what fashions that left our designers in the shade justified this influx.....anything? Mass immigration has already transformed large parts of our cities into what now look like third world bazaars; it has brought us violent crime and gang warfare, Sharia law and the burka, no-go zones and deadly terrorism. The real effects are yet to be played out, case hardening new divisions instead of encouraging integration.

Once prized British passports being dished out at the rate of 200,000 a year is a situation that could never have occurred without European regulation and outright fraud carried out by so called legal professionals under the guise of the Human Rights Act. New Labour used mass immigration as a means to destroy the traditional social structure of Britain. All the lies about jobs and growth were a smokescreen behind the party's determination to create what it's deputy leader, Harriet Harmon, called "a new social order".

What we need to realise is that post-1997 mass migration to Britain has brought us no significant benefits at all. Weighed against the future cost to our health, wealth and national security it has been an unmitigated disaster.

Blair and Brown and their political acolytes Ed's Balls and Miliband have allowed Britain to be utterly changed without ever consulting the electorate. Nobel prize-winning economist F.A. Hayek recognised the treacherous and delusional nature of politicians like Tony Blair and Gordon Brown more than 70 years ago:

"The Left intelligentsia…have so long worshipped foreign gods that they seem to have become almost incapable of seeing any good in the characteristic English institutions and traditions. That the moral values on which most of them pride themselves are largely the products of the institutions they are out to destroy, these socialists cannot, of course, admit." (4)

Only now he's gone leaving the nation in ruins can the full extent of Tony Blair's messianic recklessness and Gordon Brown's economic incompetence be exposed.

With 5.2 million foreigners arriving on our shores since 1997 and at least one million living here illegally Britain is now the most overcrowded country in western Europe.

In his book Heaven's Door, America's leading expert on migration George Borjas showed that the average immigrant's standard of living after moving from say, Somalia to Britain, improved by a staggering 300% while the benefits for the natives of that developed country were an equally staggering zero per cent. So show us the money, it's ours, how is it being spent on our behalf? No taxation without representation is the foundation and guiding principle of all democratic systems. Without it there is no political legitimacy.

No one was allowed to vote on whether we wanted more than five million people to come to live with us nor was it included in any party manifesto. Public money spent without representation is an illegitimate allocation of funds. If we knew the figures would voters not be entitled to demand a refund of these transfer payments to economic migrants? Maybe, but we'll never get to know unless we crowbar the Home Office filing cabinets, and let us hope it never comes to that.

A now unaffordable NHS is about to be privatised by the back door and public services are being erased in large swathes. So where are the figures that tell us what proportion of these cuts are needed to cope with the cost of an additional 3.2 million people using these services? We don't know, nobody does, it's a PC Secret.

Britain's annual welfare bill is now £353 billion, that's the money spent on pensions, the NHS and social security. This information is easily available from the government's own public spending website ukpublicspending.co.uk.

What we have no information about is how much of the £110 billion spent every year on social security or the £121 billion spent every year on the NHS is used up by migrants resident in the UK since 1997 and by how much this figure will increase over the next 10 years given the certainty of low to no economic growth.

Brown and his Treasury cohort Ed Balls tried to peddle the myth that foreign workers were essential because workshy Britons wouldn't work for low pay. Yet it has turned out that migrants are more likely to be benefits claimants than "lazy Brits" with ONS statistics showing a much larger percentage of immigrants claiming benefits.

Many experts now predict that the coming decades will witness uncontrollable civil unrest, poverty, strikes and violence. Before we go on to look at how this could happen one irrefutable fact needs to be absorbed. The immigration levels allowed in the last decade by New Labour has no precedent in the history of the British Isles and the traditional structure of British society will need to be irrevocably altered in order to cope with it.

That will require large amounts of money at a time when the European Union is lock-stepped into cascading economic decline with the UK an integral part of that union, and that decline.

The population of any nation that joins the EU can come to live and work in Britain as a right and the European Central Bank (ECB) is now at full stretch bailing out bankrupt nations like Greece, Ireland, Portugal, Italy and Spain.

The band-aid billions being used to buy time for this un-repayable debt has already outraged the German electorate who provide most of it and are tired of propping up member nations who have lived beyond their means for decades.

The last trillion euro fix agreed by the Euro's 17 members is doomed to fall apart as the debt mountain that is building across the Mediterranean sucks in more colossal wedges of Euro-cash. Nothing can fix Greece and the February 2012 bailout to the tune of 130 billion euros might as well have been flushed down the toilet for all the good it will do Greece in the long run. The next two years will see all of the so called PIGS (Portugal, Ireland, Greece and Spain) of Europe slide into bankruptcy, panic and in at least one case, martial law.

In Britain we will never again see growth like we did during the period 1997-2004, a one off bounty squandered by New Labour. When the BBC let loose their army of business wonks to explain what was going wrong we only got part of the story.

Yes, Wall Street corruption has sunk the system but the consequence of this collapse was that the good times were not coming back for at least another 30 years or more and that most European nations would now have to cope with excess immigrant populations which they could not reasonably support. Greedy criminal bankers had lined their pockets with money/debt raised on the value of future industrial production that would never materialise and there will be no comeback for the consumer society of old.

In this new twilight world of voodoo economics the time we have left where the paper money we get from the ATM every weekend has any value at all depends on how long those who still have their hands on the levers of power can continue to get away with the big lie that the economy is going to eventually get back to "normal". Once this lie is exposed by events: the Greek default leading to banking chaos; more bond market instability and the oil price going through the roof; the slowdown of international free trade, valueless paper currencies, confiscation of gold assets....that's the end of industrial civilisation and western democracy as we've known it, round about 2030.

Too many people have exhausted the Earth's dwindling resources too quickly and so even if we could sort out the rotten hardcore of banking criminals we still won't get our economies back growing again like they used to. The next decade will see either hyperinflation or hyper-deflation running riot throughout the capitals of Europe and there will be tremendous social upheaval, beginning with the social and economic collapse of Greece in 2013. Ireland, Portugal, Italy and Spain following hard on its heels.

That year will also see conflict in the Middle East over Iran's concealed nuclear weapons programme. It could begin with the Israeli prime minister Netanyahu authorising a ballistic missile attack on Iran's nuclear weapons facilities at Arak, Qom and Natanz resulting in Iran trying to shut down the straits of Hormuz and the industrial world's oil supply.

The other likelihood is a general conflagration of Arab states warring over what's left of Syria, with militant Islam the likely winner. The world depression following those events will be horrendous in its scope.

Assuming that war over Syria or Iran does not trigger a more general conflagration the rest of the decade will see a rapid descent in living standards. This may not happen at a consistent pace but here's how the average family will notice it. Next year there will be no foreign holiday, the year after no new car, food becomes more and more expensive, you can't afford to put the central heating on any more... and so it goes until you realise that all the money you earn has little or no value any more.

That's a best case scenario, if war in the Middle East erupts and the Straits of Hormuz are blockaded we can expect supermarkets to start running out of food within three to five days as panic buying grips the nation. Events in Europe and the Middle East are only the brooding backdrop to the domestic crisis we will face in Britain. There is now real desperation throughout the UK's private sector after long term interest rates of 0.5% have failed to encourage lending by the banks, whatever happens abroad a decade long economic decline has already begun in Britain.

Even factoring in the criminal bankers who brought the system to its knees this economic calamity could have been managed relatively peacefully and much more painlessly with population levels that were themselves declining. Immigration is the gun with which the politically correct politicians of Britain and Europe shot us all in the foot. Yet the connection between economic hardship brought on by the cost of immigration and the reduction of local services, welfare spending and NHS cuts are still concealed. In 2010 one of the first decisions made by new chancellor George Osborne was to reduce the Local Government Settlement by 25.6% over a four year spending review period, excluding spending on fire services and police. This equates to a reduction of £6.68 billion in the budgets of local authorities. When libraries, sports centres and community centres close down, when gardeners and road sweepers are laid off and graffiti reappears. When local schools close down and good schools are oversubscribed, free school meals withdrawn. Perhaps then there will be questions asked at a local level about whether these cuts have any connection to the cost of mass immigration at a national level.

What's new is the scale and suddenness of the influx of newcomers into London and our major cities. The London riots of August 2011 highlighted the emergence of gangland ghettos all over London, with residents who have no connection or sense of duty to the society in which they now live.

In most cases our laws, institutions and our religion are not theirs and never will be. Into this jobless and lawless vacuum tribal and ethnic battle grounds have been drawn up across the capital's 32 boroughs; between Somalians, Afro-Carribbeans, Muslim jihadists and East Europeans. Nearly all willing to go to war with the police when one of their own is arrested or killed.

We know who was responsible for this mess but how can we prepare for the worst that is yet to come over the next decade?

"In times of universal deceit, telling the truth becomes a revolutionary act."   **- George Orwell.**

Chapter Three
The Road To 2020

As late as May 2010 the lingering extent of New Labour's ideological commitment to changing society via mass immigration was revealed after a complaint was made to race relations investigators in Newcastle-upon-Tyne. The city was described as being "hideously white" at a conference by Neil Murphy, a Government official on secondment at Newcastle City council. Murphy may have been echoing the widely reported view expressed by Greg Dyke on taking up his post as new director-general that the BBC was "hideously white". This was the kind of remark that instantly flagged up your allegiance among the ranks of New Labour and the politically correct. Throughout New Labour's 13 years in office this self-loathing dogma became parleyed into the practical dismantling of immigration barriers over the course of successive parliaments.

First, they abolished the primary purpose rule, which had severely restricted the rights of foreign spouses to enter the country. Then the introduction of the Human Rights Act in 1998 made it impossible to stem a surge in the number of asylum seekers which rose from 1998 to over 70,000 a year.

Once Britain had signed up to the act anyone who claimed to be fleeing "unrest" could claim asylum anywhere in the EU and even if their claim was patently bogus they were allowed to remain in the UK while a lengthy appeals process rolled out at taxpayers' expense. The word "bogus" is used advisedly as most migrants claiming asylum crossed the borders of safe countries to get to Britain. Third was an avalanche of overseas student visas and work permits, which more than doubled after 1997, many of them fraudulent. In 2009 more than 228,000 students entered the country but hardly any were reported to have left Britain after their visas expired. Attempts to enforce deportation were routinely blocked by Human Rights legislation which effectively removed border control from Britain to Brussels.

What astounded many was the decision to throw open the UK labour market to new eastern European and Baltic EU states seven years before any other large EU state, and with no transitional arrangements. New Labour were wrong-footed even by the odious BNP who warned in 2004 that the lack of transitional arrangements would lead to a huge influx. New Labour said they expected no more than 30,000 Eastern European migrants would come to Britain. That virtual view of reality was farcically exposed when more than one million immigrants entered Britain from the new accession states after 2004. Every existing member of the EU erected transitional barriers except for Britain, Ireland and Sweden. The resulting influx had few positive outcomes for any of these nations.

33

Sweden, largely a homogeneous country since the Second World War now has a population where one in seven is foreign born and where new arrivals have refused to integrate or assimilate. In 2002 Swedish economist Lars Jansen said that 74% of immigrants to Sweden were living off the welfare state costing Swedish taxpayers $27 billion each year. A bastion of tolerance and once a worldwide model of social liberalism, the general election there in September 2010 saw the nation lurch right as the anti-immigrant Sweden Democrats gained the balance of power.

In Ireland the influx of immigrants failed to energize the economy, just the opposite. Ireland is now bankrupt, essentially owned by Europe's central bankers and the IMF and facing decades of austerity. Ireland is now on fast forward to a 1940s standard of living and a return to an agricultural economy. Then there's Britain.

Britain in 2011 is a society being transformed by ethnic division and certain to be the scene of violent conflict over the next decade. Before the Neather bombshell the rationale for allowing mass immigration to take place was, as expounded by New Labour, mostly economic.

In November 2003 the then home secretary, David Blunkett, speaking on BBC2's Newsnight, said that there were: "no obvious limits" to the numbers of immigrants who would be allowed to settle in the UK. Blunkett said that immigrants brought economic benefits and the (then) current inflow of more than 170,000 migrants a year was "permanently sustainable". He went further and warned that without legal migration, "growth would stall, economic flexibility and productivity would reduce".

That was official New Labour thinking at the time. Blunkett had no formal knowledge of economics, having studied politics at Sheffield University. He was typical of so many New Labour cabinet ministers with degrees in politics but with little understanding of the practical realities and hardships of the working-class communities they were elected to represent. Communities that were being asked to cope with an influx of foreigners with no homes, jobs, money or the ability to speak the English language. Other politics graduates included cabinet ministers Ruth Kelly, Jacqui Smith and Ed Miliband. Chancellor Gordon Brown didn't fall into this category, he was a history graduate.

In November 2010 Channel Four broadcast Britain's Trillion Pound Horror. During the programme various New Labour MPs were asked a simple question, how big was the national debt? None of them, including Cathy Jamieson, Rachel Reeve (now shadow chief secretary to the Treasury!) and Ian Wright knew the answer. Guesses ranged from £156 to £170 billion. A former member of the cabinet, Ben Bradshaw, not only didn't know the size of the national debt, he didn't know the difference between the budget deficit and the national debt.

Gordon Brown's tenure at No 11 and then No 10 Downing Street saw Britain's economic growth converted to a slop bucket of taxpayers' cash that was then showered on an already bloated public sector, as if it were on fire.

As of December 2011 our official national debt stands at more than 81% of our GDP. That's just government debt and means that if we added up everything the nation produced and sold in one year it would barely clear the £1 trillion plus debt mountain that is crippling Britain. This figure does not include the almost £1.2 trillion we used to bail out RBS and Lloyds which we may never get back. That's a bigger deficit than Greece, bankrupt and about to slide off a precipice towards anarchy and martial law.

However that trillion pound debt is only half the story because it does not include future pension liabilities. If we add in those that gigantic figure becomes a truly gargantuan £4.8 trillion. We need to take a moment just to think about the scale of the figures involved here. Just to count to a billion would take 30 years and to count to a trillion would take longer than recorded human history.

This is the mess Gordon Brown created as chancellor and it began with his decision to abolish Advanced Corporation Tax (ACT), which removed tax relief on share dividends, the lifeblood of private pensions. That decision left private companies struggling to make up shortfalls and forced most to wind up their final salary scheme pension funds. Brown's blunder is estimated to have nabbed the chancellor over £100 billion from the private sector while the pension schemes of the non productive public sector remained untouched. Consequently here is a fact of economic life every one of us should know, there is no money left to pay what is promised to tomorrow's pensioners, simple as that.

The burden of this debt is expected to fall on the shoulders of generations not yet born. Brown made the biggest economic gamble in history. He bet the farm that at some time in the future a return to "normal" growth cycles would wipe away the red ink on the Government's balance sheets and put most of the new migrants to work. The odds were stacked against him for reasons we shall come to, and he lost.

Because the UK is now essentially broke we are borrowing to pay our bills with the result that our national debt is increasing at a rate of £163 billion every year.

In 2010 just paying the interest alone on our national debt cost the nation £42.9 billion, that's more than £2,000 for every household in Britain and that figure is predicted to rise to £58 billion by 2015.

The accountancy firm PricewaterhouseCoopers have predicted that the UK's total debt may exceed £10 trillion by 2015, that's roughly 507% of its GDP, which makes us not only bankrupt but the second most indebted nation on Earth, behind Ireland. One can only imagine the despair coursing through Prime Minister David Cameron as he surveys the wreckage from within an uneasy coalition pact. The next generations' pockets have already been picked clean. He can't even raise extra cash by selling off gold because of Gordon Brown's crackpot decision to junk a third of Britain's gold reserves at $260 an once, (gold is worth more than $1800 an once as I am writing this) a decision that cost the country billions.

If we add up all the money collected in tax from all the working people in Britain for one year it would not be enough to pay for what we now spend on the welfare state.

In 2008/09, UK gross income tax receipts were £152.5 billion and in that same year UK welfare benefits cost the taxpayer £150.1 billion, so we had £2.4 billion left for everything else; defence, the justice system, the NHS, the roads and railways, Europe, old peoples' homes, winter fuel payments …the list goes on. All the goodies that make Britain a civilised society. The rest we had to borrow.

It got worse in 2009/10, when the Treasury took in only £140.5 billion in gross income tax receipts against social security benefit costs of £164.7 billion. For the first time in our history we spent more on social security than we collected in taxes.

For Cameron to even chip away at this mountain of tick he would have to get rid of the entire social security system and that deficit figure will be greater next year given a growth rate of only 0.7%. (1)

Yet the problem is bigger, much bigger. Even if we lost all of the thousands of non-jobs created by New Labour and all of its quango's and sacked all the useless social workers and teachers and then all the corrupt and inept bankers then let all the banks draining our money away go bust, it is still nowhere near enough. The cuts needed to balance the books must still go deeper, much deeper.

It would normally be the job of the governor of the bank of England to steady the ship of state with reassuring words of seeing light at the end of the tunnel but such is the extent of the disaster that closes in on the nation's finances that Sir Mervyn King reflected in 2011 that Britain now faces "a full blown systemic crisis". A leading Sunday newspaper reported that: "his response to George Osborne's admission that there will be six years of austerity to pay down the deficit was said to be, 'More like 60 years'." (2)

What Sir Mervyn King is hinting at is that almost all public spending would have to go in order to stop borrowing sinking the nation, all of the welfare state: that's all unemployment benefit, sickness benefit, housing benefit, tax credits, social housing subsidy, social services, residential care for the elderly, libraries, the basic state pension, winter fuel allowances, pensioners' bus passes.... these are all unaffordable given our current financial crisis, and that doesn't include the NHS which costs £121 billion a year and is now being run on the state equivalent of credit card debt.

Hell, what cuts anyway? The Coalition's much derided cuts do not add up to a drop in the ocean of debt that has engulfed us. The Coalition cannot afford to tell the truth and be voted out of office by a fearful and then panicking public unable to face the awful reality of our situation so the public must remain in fearful limbo, ignorant of the national emergency that engulfs us.

The mess we've been left by New Labour needs to be explained in terms the man in the street can understand because the media has failed to convey the basic economic facts of life. When an economic forecaster comes on air and waffles on about GDP how many viewers reach for the remote? Yet this is vital stuff, it's your money that has been water-cannoned down the drain.

GDP stand for Gross Domestic Product and it is the market value of all the goods and services produced by Britain in one year. In 2009/10 the value of everything we made in Britain was just over £1.7 trillion, incidentally that's less than the £1.9 trillion of liability Sir Fred Goodwin managed to rack up as he bankrupted RBS. No-one in the history of banking lost money faster than Sir Fred Goodwin and no-one wasted taxpayers' money faster than his pal, Gordon Brown. Largely because of Gordon Brown's spending spree Britain is more than £1trillion in debt and the ONS say that this debt will increase to £1.3 trillion by 2013.

GDP is the total value of all the goods and services produced in Britain in one year. Everything we make and sell or export minus everything we need but don't produce ourselves, imports. That's GDP. If we sell more than we buy we have a surplus or growth. The way economists look at how rich or poor we are is by dividing the value of everything we produce by the number of people who

39

produce it. That's when we find out what we can afford to pay ourselves without borrowing. At a projected growth rate of 0.7% in 2012 we can afford just about nothing. The whole public sector is unaffordable as the money to pay for it comes from growth and 0.7% doesn't go a long way. The announcement of more than half a million jobs to go in the public sector is only the tip of the iceberg as all public sector jobs are unaffordable at those rates of growth.

Yet this is only the visible debt, when you dig deeper the situation is much, much worse. One of the UK's foremost investment analysts, Michael Saunders from CitiGroup, has calculated our 'external debt' – ie, what Britain owes the rest of the world and has concluded that it is not 81% but 400% of GDP, the highest in the G7 by some margin. The next down, France, has an overall external debt of 176% of GDP while America has a debt ratio of almost 100%.

In 2012 just the interest paid on our national debt cost the country £47.6 billion a year which is about the cost of the whole education budget. What's our individual share of the bill? According to the Office for Budget Responsibility if you're in work it's more than £26,000 for every family in Britain but taxes raised per family are only £21,300 so to meet the shortfall we are borrowing nearly £5000 for every working family in Britain every year. That's what we owe now, but the real shocker is what we need to pay out in the future. This colossal interest payment is expected to jump to £65.5 billion in 2016-17. Britain needs a growth rate of approximately 3% per year just to keep unemployment where it is now so how many more will join the dole queues at a predicted growth rate of 0.7% now and an average well below 3% over the rest of the decade?

Research produced for investment bank Morgan Stanley by Haver Analytics in 2011 showed that if we include household debt into the mix of GDP to debt ratio we find that Britain is by far the most indebted nation on earth with 950% compared to Europe's 500% and the US at 440%. That means that for every £1 we make in the UK, everything we produce to sell in one year, we still owe out £10 to pay for our public services and to continue running the economy. Thus we are getting further and further into debt as the economy slows to a halt.

That's the real legacy of "iron" chancellor Gordon Brown but one solution he never considered was just letting the banks go bust. Who said that would have been a disaster?....Gordon Brown did. If we had done that could things be any worse that they are now? Lack of demand and lack of capital will be written on the tombstone of the UK economy in 2013 and RBS will be just as bankrupt then as it is now so what would have been lost by just handing over the £31,000 every household in Britain was charged to bail out the banks and letting them use their own cash to stimulate a recovery?

RBS would still be have been open for business, it would just be its shareholders or unsecured creditors who would have had to take the hit. RBS could then have been sold off to the highest bidder, even if the bid was for just 10 quid. This would have at least put an end to the obscenity of RBS senior management still rewarding themselves £500 million worth of bonuses from the public purse while the taxpayer continues to prop up the biggest dead duck in corporate history.

The money Gordon Brown wasted by pouring it into RBS could have provided a massive boost to industry and jobs. It won't happen now because the banksters who run the finance houses won't allow it and so RBS is on the way down faster than the Titanic, along with the rest of our banking sector when the next European sovereign debt nation after Greece, most likely Italy, defaults. And then it gets really grim.

The only nation with the money to bail out the Spanish or Italian economies are the Germans and the European Central Bank. It would mean that the industrious German taxpayer would again have to transfer crippling amounts of their national wealth to fund the laxity of the average Greek, Italian or Spaniard in the hope that structural reform in the future would magically transform laid back Mediterranean loafers into productive Germans. Of course the working habits of generations of Greeks cannot be changed without forced coercion and so any new bailout will only put off the day of reckoning by another year or two. Yet it seems that this is the best we can hope for before calamity in Greece circa 2013 at the latest. Greece is now on the verge of outright civil war as political divisions of the far left and right harden. What is happening today in Greece will be repeated in Britain after 2015 when we will be in a worse financial position than they are, our AAA status removed and unable to even go a begging for ECB money to bail us out. The British economy having crossed the event horizon of national debt under Gordon Brown can only buy time on more borrowed money until we are sucked into a fiscal black hole that will lead to our own chaos and civil unrest.

While in government New Labour had the chance to insulate itself from this nightmare by paying down its debts during the early years of surplus from 1997 to 2004 but the burden of immigration has wiped away the safety net that was the British welfare state and the NHS. The cost of future old age pensions may be as high as £1.4 trillion say the ONS, the cost of public sector pensions for teachers, social workers, civil servants.. £1.2 trillion, the cost of bailing out the banks £1.2 trillion... all in all the ONS say we need to find an extra £3.8 trillion on top of the one trillion we owe already to meet our obligations. Gordon Brown must have been aware of this potential spending black hole but still allowed a million more immigrants to come and live in Britain during his two year stint at No 10.

So, fast forward to November 29, 2011 and chancellor George Osborne is standing up in Parliament and announcing that the annual public spending deficit, (that's more borrowed money necessary in order to continue to pay ourselves a welfare state and NHS we can no longer afford), will be increased by £111 billion over the next five years. That's on top of the rise announced in October 2010 from £697 billion to £757 billion by 2014. As of 2011 we officially have a bigger budget deficit than bankrupt Greece and even those economists who exclude external debt calculations fear that by 2015 the size of the UK national debt could be 507% of GDP. By that date the UK's AAA status will be long gone and there will be the beginning of a seemingly endless crisis with a huge population of permanently jobless new citizens relying on a bankrupted state to feed and house them. The Coalition are hoping and praying that economic growth will pull us out of this quicksand but it's a mighty big "if".

After 2015 oil production will begin to permanently decline and there will be no denying that traditional cycles of industrial growth have gone forever to be replaced by a steady and then accelerating contraction of living standards. At that point expect massive propaganda telling us we have nothing to worry about and that renewable energy will save the day. We will remain in limbo for a few brief years until the next big domestic crisis wakes up an outraged electorate who will finally demand answers. The student loan protests are a pinprick compared to the bloodbath to come (I wrote this before the London riots but the situation continues to accelerate).

In denial of the facts PC Europe's knee-jerk response is to throw more money at the banks, but there is no amount of money on Earth that will save the Greeks from complete meltdown and a forced march back to an agrarian economy. The most likely scenario is a new crisis brought on when the stopgap re-capitalisation of the ECB is unpicked by market forces by the end of 2013.

What about the world economic downturn, isn't that to blame for everything? Japan has been going through an economic crisis for the last 20 years. Without any natural energy resources like North Sea oil to prop it up.

The downturn that began there in 1989 has continued to this day but because a smaller GDP is being divided up among a falling population Japan is surviving and prospering. Average incomes are rising faster than those in Europe because Japan has not allowed mass immigration. It remains a homogenous society as we saw from the orderly way its citizens behaved after the Fukushima crisis.

There was no violence, queues for food and water were good natured and calm. Japan's so called lost decades of economic decline since 1989 were cushioned by vast export surpluses from the 1980's and no accumulated household debt.

Japan's high tech firms have remained in Japanese hands but more importantly the division of GDP among a declining population means that it will remain a stable society. In 2011 Japan exported £140 billion worth of advanced manufacturing to China and their unemployment rate stands at 4.5% and falling compared to Britain's 8.3%

and rising. Britain has neither that financial cushion nor Japan's world class high tech exports…or a society without the "benefits" of mass immigration.

With the prospect of at least a decade with little or no growth and a population that's increasing faster than anywhere else in Europe the prospects for UK plc look desperate. During the next decade we will see the financial implosion of the British economy as our massive and worsening debt to GDP ratio, like the Balrog, drags Britain down the Crack of Doom.

After we had borrowed up to 240% of GDP to finance the war against Hitler it took us until 1969 to reduce that debt to 60% of GDP. We were saved by North Sea oil but that's been and gone now and there's nothing to fill the gap. We make next to nothing, three quarters of our economy is made up of the service sector…that means shopping, fast food and public sector workers who contribute nothing to the balance of payments.

It may have been the Thatcher administration who first deregulated the banking system but it was Gordon Brown and his wingman Ed Balls who carried on the work of the Thatcherite right leaving the banks free to make loans to anyone who could type their name on an online credit card application: it was their system of slack financial regulation that divided the Treasury, Bank of England and the Financial Services Authority (FSA) in 2000. Their new system failed to spot the housing bubble coming over the hill or the massive fraud swirling around mortgage lending and credit default scams from US investment banks.

Those already doomed American banks were eagerly joined in the trough of funny money by the snouts of RBS investment "experts" like Fred Goodwin who insanely pressed on with the £27 billion takeover of Dutch dead duck ABN Amro bank without even examining its overcooked books, riddled with bad sub-prime mortgage paper. The US financial sector was in a state of panic over sub prime well before the Dutch deal was sealed but still Goodwin ploughed on, the banking world's biggest ever sap, (see The Big Short by Michael Lewis) oblivious to the biggest financial crisis of our age even as it was unfolding under his nose.

Goodwin racked up losses of £24.1 billion while in charge of RBS but still walked away with a company pension of £693,000 a year (reduced to £340,000 later on), and a knighthood (later removed).

The Commons Treasury Select Committee's report on the collapse of Northern Rock said that the FSA had "systematically failed in its duty" to oversee the bank's activities, but the FSA was a global laughing stock way before the Rock's collapse due to its inability to check up on or regulate anything bigger than a cheque with the wrong date on it. Just how lax the system was that New Labour spawned can be illustrated by any number of examples combining unregulated banking with unrestricted immigration.

In 2009 Albanian Krenar Lusha, 30, was given £93,000 after NatWest failed to complete full checks on his UK status. That's a 100% mortgage, no deposit no security, there you go…enjoy. With gratitude in check Lusha wasted no time and spent the money on a house in Derby which he used to stash bomb-making equipment. It turned out that Lusha was an Al-Qaeda terrorist who had sneaked into Britain hidden on a lorry. No kidding. His illegal status didn't stop him from getting a £30,000-a-year engineering job or a driving licence. The bank even offered him a second mortgage! (3)

New Labour's unofficial mouthpiece, the BBC, could not prevent an investigation into a network of bent mortgage brokers dishing out dodgy home loans from surfacing in 2008. In a rare piece of non PC investigative enquiry a BBC online team were contacted by three former trainee mortgage advisers employed by the London Professional Academy (LPA) based at an office block in Barking. The company was owned by Ghanaian businessman San Morre.

The BBC reported that "The trainees were sent to various companies including - CMS Mortgages - which operated from LPA's headquarters during 2007. While at CMS Mortgages the former trainees allege that they were instructed to falsify the passport details of foreign nationals, instructed to put down British in the nationality box on mortgage application forms if the client was a foreign national, instructed to get chartered accountants to create ghost companies and incomes to make low paid, foreign clients look like prime borrowers." (4).

Those who can get out would be well advised to start making plans now as the clock is ticking extremely fast.

"A lie told often enough becomes the truth." - Lenin

Chapter Four
Beyond The Fix

So why did we need more than five million immigrants, and given the current rate of unemployment why are immigrants still pouring into the country at a rate of 239,000 a year at the last count?

Somewhere along the line New Labour's mantra about diversity became a hope that migrants would exert a downward pressure on wages and increase the tax base. What New Labour got desperately wrong or refused to recognise (because their aim was to change society rather than the economy), was that although some skilled migrants do indeed bring economic benefit to the UK their contribution to the economy is counter balanced by their addition to the population. They live here so they need the NHS, pensions, housing.... just like everyone else.

Baron Glasman now free to fess up to New Labour's immigration disaster admits that mass immigration served as an "unofficial wages policy".

Glasman now points to New Labour as being responsible for a generation of far right populism manifested in the growth of the EDL and also professes alarm at the "hate and rage against us from working class people who have always been true to Labour". Well he might now his career on New Labour's political front line is over. (1)

As almost every first year economics undergraduate knows, cheap labour is good for providing short term growth to an economy at a longer term cost to the taxpayer. Longer term growth would need wages at a permanently low level for those low wages to have no additional costs associated with them, like healthcare.

For that kind of scenario look at low-wage economies like China or further back in time to Nazi Germany, the Confederate states of America or Victorian England for that matter. That kind of labour is rightly anathema to our modern liberal democracies and can only exist in repressive societies.

What about cheap labour in the modern world? Dr. Donald Huddle, a Rice University economics professor, published a systematic analysis of the costs associated with illegal workers who may increase short-term profits for employers but at a huge eventual cost to the taxpayer.

His study looked at the effects of an amnesty for illegal workers in America. Huddle found that: "Most illegal aliens have low educational attainment, few skills, and they work for low wages, often in the underground economy where they pay no taxes on their earnings. Since about three million illegal aliens gained legal status in the [US] amnesty of 1986, the flow of illegal immigration has increased, and today that population is estimated at 9-11 million illegal alien residents in the country. The former Immigration and Naturalization Service estimated that the illegal alien population was increasing by about half a million aliens per year in 2000."

Huddle's investigations found that at that time of the study (1996), that: "the illegal alien population was estimated to be about five million persons. The estimated fiscal cost of those illegal aliens to the federal, state and local governments was about $33 billion. This impact was partially offset by an estimated $12.6 billion in taxes paid to the federal, state and local governments, resulting in a net cost to the American taxpayer of about $20 billion every year. This estimate did not include indirect costs that result from unemployment payments to Americans who lost their jobs to illegal aliens willing to work for lower wages. Nor did it include lost tax collections from those American workers who became unemployed. The study estimated those indirect costs from illegal immigration at an additional $4.3 billion annually." (2).

Now factor in the passage of time. The children of those illegals need to go to school, need medical assistance, social care, judicial and correctional contact. Between 1996 and 2004 the illegal alien population would have roughly doubled so that the cost to the American taxpayer would rise to $70 billion.

The warning was there for New Labour, if anyone had wanted to take notice. The argument for mass immigration on economic terms was unanswerable....loud and clear the report said that those countries who allowed it would pay dearly in the longer term. The additional costs of educating the children of immigrants in Britain has been estimated at £7.6bn a year, this is a huge sum if we are to assume that a large percentage of these children will never find work in a permanently contracting British economy. The Huddle Study was hugely influential in the world of international labour studies, but not in the world of Blair/Brown's New Labour experiment to socially re-engineer Britain.

As an aid in its quest to make the transition to a multicultural Britain as smooth as possible New Labour enacted laws that allowed political correctness to gain a stranglehold over all sections of the public services: schools, hospitals and local authorities. Political correctness and unwarranted accusations of racism meant no one was willing to ask the question almost everyone wanted to hear the answer to. Why did we let more than five million people and their families move permanently into our overcrowded island in such a short space of time?

Where once the intellectual was asked for opinions that would become the barometer of debate, people like Labour's respected former chancellor Denis Healy, New Labour's PC laws facilitated the triumph of the superficial.

Tony Blair and his inner circle lapped up celebrity culture where the vacuous utterances of Eddie Izzard or Emma Thompson soon came to set the agenda of what was permissible to say in order to stay within PC boundaries. What used to pass for open debate soon became the glib presentation of personal feelings and experiences preferred to any logical presentation of facts.

The first major inquiry to address the true economic value of immigration into the UK was a report published by the House of Lords in 2008, The Economic Impact of Immigration. Evidence was taken from hundreds of experts who concluded that "any economic benefits are unlikely to bear comparison with its substantial impact on population growth".

The Economic Affairs Committee of the House of Lords concluded that: "The overall fiscal impact of immigration is likely to be small," in other words of no great value to the public purse and went on to say that: "we have found no evidence for the argument, made by the government, business and many others, that net immigration - immigration minus emigration - generates significant economic benefits for the existing UK population." (3)

The committee had among its members two former chancellors, a former governor of the Bank of England and many distinguished economists and industrialists. Experts who systematically demolished New Labour's fiscal arguments about immigration being good for the economy.

New Labour claims that immigration was needed to support the provision of pensions and care for the elderly were also found to be fake.

At the turn of the millennium, an ageing population was common to all the world's advanced economies. The empowerment of women, more liberty and leisure time and equal opportunities had led to the control of fertility, leading to low birth rates, and declines in mortality. The number of young people in society fell but more folk survived to old age. It was the young who would need to support them.

The number of younger people of working age for each person of pensionable age is called the Potential Support Ratio (PSR). At the moment in European countries it stands at about four. That is four young people in work helping pay for the retirement benefits of one elderly person. Countries with relatively high birth rates such as the UK, France and the Scandinavian countries can expect lower levels of population ageing than Germany, Italy and Greece which (at that time) had much lower birth rates. Most immigrants tend to be young men aged 18 to 34, and at first their arrival does reduce the average age of the population so at first there's slightly more than a four to one ratio. But to maintain that slightly better ratio you need to constantly allow in more and more immigrants and this leads to a huge growth in the overall population.

So what happens to all those new immigrants when they age? The answer is that yet more immigrants are needed. To keep the four plus to one ratio would require the population of the UK to increase to 119 million by 2051 and to 303 million by the end of the century. (4) At that stage we would all be living like maggots and any notion of a civilised existence would be finished.

More and more people churning more and more money round the economy does not increase the GDP per head of population, it only makes that country more and more crowded in the long run, not any better off. The way to tackle pensions was a no-brainer as far as the House of Lords committee was concerned, not unlimited immigration but an increase in the retirement age.

The Prime Minister, David Cameron knows this and has proposed the retirement age be increased to 66 at the earliest opportunity. Even the French have now cottoned on to the fact that immigration is not needed to cope with French citizens who live longer and have raised their retirement age, to 62. Of course we are in far more trouble than France in respect of immigration difficulties long term.

Cameron's government know that the retirement age will have to keep on rising and that for some better off sections of society it will go altogether. And if you're 10 years from retirement now, and have paid class 1 contributions all your life you have a right to be worried, and resentful. Retirement age was lifted to 66 in George Osborne's autumn statement, some economists are already saying that must rise to 74, others are aware that the basic state pension is now unaffordable.

Yet another reason for allowing mass immigration given by New Labour was that the white working class refused to fill low paid vacancies advertised in job centres. Yet, as countless surveys have since proved, this was because Britain's benefits system made signing off illogical for claimants who would be made worse off by taking a job. New Labour never once considered reforming the welfare system or raising the minimum wage to a level which would make doing the "dirty" jobs palatable to even those considered workshy.

Only now that New Labour are out of office are the facts about the impact of immigration coming to light. On January 10, 2012 the Governments Migration Advisory Committee (MAC) which was set up by New Labour published a report that nailed as false the New Labour assertion that immigration boosts economic growth.

The report found that claim to be entirely bogus because the benefits of any growth goes to immigrants themselves and not the indigenous population. The report also confirmed that one British job was lost for every four non-EU workers arriving in Britain between 2005 and 2010. MAC also found that foreign workers do indeed take jobs that would have gone to British workers, more than 160,000 between 2005 and 2010 and that immigration pushed up the costs of housing and education but there was no breakdown of how much these costs came to in total.

The chairman of MAC, Professor David Metcalf, said that low wage British workers were being undermined by immigration and that British public services were deteriorating under the strain. Again, no mention of the exact cost of the extra strain being leveraged on public services.

Eventually some public servant, sickened by all the secrecy and hypocrisy, may have the guts to reveal what these extra costs decimating the economy add up to but right now there are still only clues available, like ONS statistics showing that the cost of providing working age benefits have gone up by 90% since 1997. Osborne's autumn statement revealed that unemployment would rise from 8.1% in 2010 to 8.7% in 2012, after that who knows?

By 2015 it's crunch time for UK plc; the seeds sown by New Labour's profligacy will finally bear down on all of us as the national debt approaches £10 trillion and we are spending more than three quarters of everything we earn as a nation servicing that debt. Nobody in the Coalition has a clue what will happen after 2015, some will be praying for a miracle. What we do know is that there are more than a million 16-24 year olds out of work right now but at the same time we are required to absorb yet another wave of 239,000 immigrants post-2010 and the same again in 2011. Even if the economy was to recover and create thousands of new jobs how many of these would go to native British workers?

The Work and Pensions secretary Iain Duncan Smith seems to be the only cabinet minister willing to look realistically at the sheer scale of the crisis but sounded near to despair when he begged British firms to "give a chance" to unemployed young British workers rather than relying on cheap foreign labour.

In an age of global overpopulation and a world commodity shortage it's barely credible that the UK is not allowed to give preference to its own workforce because of European labour laws. While we remain in the EU any jobs created by building new houses or railways or other infrastructure projects using taxpayers' money will go to mostly foreign labour. There can be no sympathy for public sector unions, on strike for a share of public money that no longer exits. They are the architects of their own downfall. As the nation's coffers bleed dry to service the needs of a standing army of jobless foreign workers they must rue the day they allowed Tony Blair to get rid of the union block vote, a bulwark that once protected the working-class of England.

If socialism ever meant anything, surely it was the maintenance and support of social cohesion within the working-class. A cohesion traditionally dependent upon the willingness of that community to find strength in common values and make sacrifices for each other.

The slogan muttered by Gordon Brown before his 2010 general election defeat about "British Jobs for British Workers" must now have the union rank and file choking on its home made beer as they head off to claim jobseekers' allowance.

What actually happened was that the new low-paid jobs created by New Labour went to foreign workers while the low status, low-paid jobs remained unfilled.

As MigrationWatch's Sir Andrew Green said: "Immigration has little effect on vacancies. We had 600,000 vacancies in 2001 when the Government first gave this as a reason for expanding immigration and we still have a similar number, despite net immigration of roughly 900,000 in the same period. The reason is that the number of jobs in an economy isn't fixed. Immigrants also create demand and thus extra vacancies, so there is no end to the cycle. It would be much better if employers trained British workers rather than importing them from abroad. They could also try paying a decent wage to the unskilled, whose pay is being held down by the current large-scale immigration. No wonder some employers are happy." (5)

The governments own Labour Force Survey showed that the number of adults under-25 out of work in December 2011 was more than one million or 20.4%, the highest level of youth unemployment since records began. Overall there were 2.5 million people out of work in the UK at the end of 2010 but in the chancellor's autumn statement we learned that figure will increase by 220,000 to 2.77 million by 2012. That's almost the same number of immigrants still arriving each year. At this point we need to ask the question again, why were 5.2 million immigrants allowed to settle in the UK and why are more still arriving?

If Sir Andrew Green had been tempted to say "I told you so" to Gordon Brown he resisted but what he did tell a national newspaper in 2011 was this: "Over a million students in one year, with no interviews before arrival and no checks on departures; and a points-based system that has increased immigration not reduced it. This is what they called 'managed migration'. It would be hard to imagine after 13 years in charge a more shambolic inheritance." (6)

Under New Labour over 40% of all young people were sent to university and the outcome was a ferocious dumbing down of standards. Employers complained that skill shortages were worse than ever and were forced to recruit migrants to fill the gap. Gordon Brown wanted the economy to expand but didn't want the wage inflation that traditionally accompanied it. Foreign workers would do the trick and a massive influx were given access all areas to the UK in an act of unprecedented political expediency without a care for the long term fallout.

Labour's new leader Ed Miliband claims it is a myth to blame Britain's huge budget deficit on his party and if you exclude any reference to immigration it is just possible to make a case that after the credit crunch tax revenues did collapse and so the treasury lost revenue, increasing the cost of public spending. Yet just how much of public spending under New Labour was used solely to pay for the juggernaut of mass immigration, and what percentage of the national cake is still funding illegal immigrants' access to the welfare state, NHS, housing, social services... and what will be the cost over the next 30 years? Such is the power of PC that no one in Westminster has the courage to ask or answer this question. The budget in March 2012 is expected to announce that every taxpayer is to be given a personal tax statement detailing how all their tax money is spent. What will not be present on the chancellor's pie chart is any breakdown of what proportion of that tax expenditure is the extra cost of immigration since 1997. What Brown and Blair left the nation was the shambles of an unasked for population explosion that will overwhelm us within a generation, ravaging our social infrastructure and making the indigenous white British a minority within their children's lifetimes. The very least the Labour leadership can do is now admit that throughout their time in government they lied to the country about the benefits of immigration, and show us where the money went.

No sensible person would deny that a constant flow of the brightest and the best immigrants into Britain, regardless of race, is essential to keep on revitalising the economy. As a child my heroes weren't selected on the basis of colour: Mohammed Ali, Pele, Stevie Wonder, George Best and the Beatles crossed all boundaries. It had to do with intelligence, talent and charisma, not with being a specific colour. Mass immigration has brought huge changes to Britain that have been made in our name but without legitimacy. Time passes quickly and what seems like unimportant decisions can have enormous repercussions, without most people even noticing.

Suddenly, over the course of a decade or two what would have seemed outrageous gradually becomes unchangeable, permanent. All we can do now is watch it all play out as an endless austerity eats away at the fabric of our nation.

"The lack of money is the root of all evil."

- Mark Twain.

Chapter 5
We'll Have To Go On Paying

One of the experts who made submissions to the House of Lords Committee in 2008 was David Coleman, Professor of Demographics at Oxford University.

He calculated that New Labour's open door immigration policy was costing taxpayers £7.8 billion a year, about £350 a year for each taxpayer in Britain. That was in 2007, when net immigration to Britain was a million less than it is today. Professor Coleman's figures are the most accurate estimates we have about the cost of immigration to date.

In 2007 Coleman calculated that of this £7.8 billion immigration tax £4 billion was needed annually to cope with the increased cost of immigrant crime, £1.6 billion for asylum support and processing and £330 million to treat illnesses such as HIV.

In 2010 MigrationWatchUK estimated that there were 1.1million illegal immigrants in the UK using the NHS, social services, receiving housing benefit etc and if an amnesty were given to each illegal immigrant and he/she then found a permanent job on minimum wage it would still cost the taxpayer £220,000 to support each, now legal immigrant, over the course of their lifetime.

Most shocking was MigrationWatchUK research showing that: "For an unemployed immigrant the estimated Lifetime Costs are £660,000 for a single person and £1,030,000 for a two child family." (1)

Just take in that figure in for a second.... more than £1 million per family must be found by the taxpayer to pay for one illegal immigrant family's lifetime of unemployment. So surely we now need to know as a matter of urgency how many of the 5.2 million new legal immigrants are unemployed so we can make the calculation of how much this is all costing. Unfortunately there are no such figures to be had. Political correctness and the fear of an anti-immigration backlash serves to keep the lid on this most sensitive statistic, this being a scandal of the greatest fiscal magnitude. The "total lifetime" cost referred to by MigrationWatchUK covers a 25-year-old immigrant who works for the minimum wage, marries, has two children, does not have a pension and so in retirement receives a Pension Credit, and lives throughout in private rented housing. Their calculations take these costs from the date of marriage at age 25 through 40 years of work to retirement at 65 years of age and then 15 years of retirement.

So how much? Without the statistical information to go on we can only make back of the envelope calculations but MigrationWatchUK say we need to find an extra £12.8 billion a year just for those immigrants here legally.

61

The MigrationWatchUK statistic is based on ONS figures showing immigrants now comprising 12% of the workforce with a male unemployment rate of one in ten, and is a conservative estimate. I say conservative because this figure does not include the million or more illegal immigrants who have access to the NHS, social services, and housing benefit. It could be double or ten times that amount. That's anything from £12.8 to £128 billion a year and the public need to know the facts.

In MigrationWatchUK News, May 4, 2009, it was reported that: "An immigrant couple living on the minimum wages who then retire on Pension Credit, will receive Housing Benefit and Council Tax Benefit throughout their working life and throughout their retirement. The total Housing Benefit they receive will be £291,000 plus a further £19,000 in Council Tax Benefit."

The Coalition government under David Cameron probably knows by now that they will have to find at least an extra £12 to £13 billion a year just to deal with the increasing burden of immigrant unemployed as well as working immigrants and their dependants. That would be more than enough to pay the tuition fees of all British students who wanted to go to university and restore the maintenance grant, clear the NHS deficit, give free travel and subsidised heating for all pensioners, stop all library closures and finance new high speed rail investment as far as the north east of England that could provide massive levels of employment putting Britain in the best possible position to meet the coming energy crisis. With no growth in the economy and as the migrant population boom gathers pace this decade that £13 billion a year will balloon out of sight. Watch what is happing on the streets of Athens in 2012 because the same turmoil will be everywhere in

Britain by 2016, a nation in the midst of a violent struggle with London at the epicentre.

What happened under New Labour was the rolling out of the welcome mat to the world's poor in a vainglorious parade of social conscience made in the context of their paralysing fear of being seen as racist. The spurious logic that this mass influx was needed to solve a manpower shortage has been exposed as a lie.

It is estimated that more than 73% of all recent immigrants live in London. When the new Prime Minister, David Cameron, announced on October 26, 2010, that no one would be able to receive more than £400 per week in housing benefit as a way of staunching escalating outflows of taxpayers' cash the Mayor of London, Boris Johnson, said he would not accept: "Kosovo-style social cleansing" in the capital, which would see thousands of poorer families forced out by benefit reforms.

Of course Boris Johnson faces re-election for his position of London's mayor and his outburst was intended to put pressure on the Prime Minister, already under pressure from his LibDem partners, who had advocated an amnesty for illegal immigrants in their manifesto.

Liberal Democrats have claimed that around 200,000 people could be driven out of areas with high rents as a result of the drive to reduce the cost of housing benefit. What was not raised by either the Prime Minister nor the leader of the opposition is the fact that the vast majority of these 200,000 families are recent immigrants, many of them without work.

Take just one group of the recently arrived, Somalis. The Government has no reliable statistics on how many Somalis now live in Britain. One official reckoned that there were 150,000 legal Somalis and three times as many illegal ones. They live mostly in London but there are sizeable numbers living in Liverpool, Sheffield, Bristol, Cardiff and other English cities.

This is the biggest Somali community living anywhere outside of Somalia in the world. Of all the Somalis who have entered Britain since 1997 around 81% are unemployed and have extremely low levels of education, many of them are illiterate even in their own language.

A 2008 report by the Institute for Public Policy Research said that 46% of Somalis had arrived in Britain since 2000 and that 48% had no qualifications and barely a quarter of those of working age was employed — those who were mostly had menial jobs. In 1997 Haringey Council found that 50.6% of its Somali adults were illiterate in any language.

The Somali community is fractured, has failed to integrate and has lost its traditional social structures. What it does still retain is a strong connection with Islam and a disconnection with the civic structures of its newly adopted homeland.

Britain has only one Somali mayor, in Tower Hamlets, East London. Many young Somalis become part of gangs like the Tottenham Somalis, the Woolwich Boys or Thug Farm. Two Somali brothers, Mustaf and Yusuf Jama, murdered PC Sharon Beshenivsky during a robbery in Bradford in 2005. Many others become radicalised by Islam. Two of the four men who tried to bomb the London Underground on July 21, 2005, were Somali asylum-seekers. If we take MigrationWatchUK's estimate of the lifetime costs of an unemployed immigrant just this one ethnic group are using up vast amounts of taxpayer resources as 80% of Somalis live in social housing compared with just 17% of indigenous UK residents and £1billion a year more is going to be needed to pay for immigrant social housing over the next 10 years.

Even if each Somali worked for 40 years on minimum wage they would still be eligible for pension credits on retirement as well as council tax benefit and housing benefit on the way, at a cost to the taxpayer of more than £310,000 for each Somali, a mammoth bill for immigration yet to arrive and one that is going to break Britain financially.

Surely taxpayers have a right to know how much of their deductions are going to pay for these new arrivals? A good guess would be at least £500 per year for each and every standard rate taxpayer in Britain, that's at the moment.

If this sort of news ever got out do you doubt that many of the silent majority would begin demanding, why should we pay? After all, no one ever asked the electorate if they wanted these people to come and live here and, as it turns out, there was no logical economic cause.

New Labour leader Ed Miliband's reaction to the reduction of rent subsidies to a still generous £400 a week, that's £21,000 a year, was transmitted via his shadow minister for work and pensions Karen Buck who, ignoring statistics showing the government facing the biggest financial crisis since the 1930s, stated: "they don't want black women, they don't want ethnic minority women and they don't want Muslim women living in central London. They just don't." (2)

At this juncture we must conclude that she is in denial or just wilfully ignorant of the basic economic facts, as, by proxy, must be Ed Miliband. It seems that Labour still won't /cannot acknowledge the cost of its own immigration disaster.

Even before their defeat at the 2010 election the magnitude of New Labour's error had begun to ring alarm bells. After 2008 chancellor Alastair Darling finally began to see economic reality hurtling towards him like a runaway train.

His April 2009 budget revealed that Britain's national debt would reach £1.7 trillion, equivalent to 80% of the nation's GDP. That's 80% of everything produced by every factory and worker in the country. Yet that figure was still a gross underestimate of the nation's indebtedness, deliberately failing, as we have seen, to take account of £3.8 trillion worth of pension promises.

The unprecedented borrowing programme then undertaken by New Labour meant that future generations of British workers would have to face higher taxes in order to pay off that debt but in return for what? No pension, no welfare state, no university education for their kids? What would you do, work for nothing? It seems unlikely and on a macro scale also raises doubts about international investors' willingness to go on lending to the UK long term.

It turned out to be even worse than forecast, since Mr Darling had based his borrowing plans on an assumption that the UK economy would be booming again by 2011, an assumption most fiscal analysts believed to be overly optimistic. They were right, figures published on 26 January 2010, showed Britain limping out of recession with a growth rate of 0.1%, well below official forecasts at the time of 0.4%. New Labour budget projections said that public-sector net debt, the amount of outstanding government borrowing, would reach £1,370 billion in 2013/14.

When Labour took office in 1997, the national debt, how much the country owes, was £356 billion. In May 2010 when New Labour's chief secretary to the Treasury Liam Byrne signed off with a note to his successor telling him: "Dear Chief Secretary. I'm afraid to tell you there is no money. Kind regards and good luck!" the national debt had increased to almost £1 trillion. Byrne must have thought this was all quite funny and his flippant attitude had no doubt served him well in his previous position, as immigration minister.

It is true that Britain could not have avoided the global recession entirely, but the New Labour Government could have massively mitigated our present plight by exercising restraint in public spending and responsible regulation of the banks and their ilk.

The reckless spending is easily demonstrated: New Labour ran a surplus for each of their first four years of government so by 2001 Britain was in the black to the tune of £37.8 billion. They did this by sticking to the spending plans inherited from Conservative chancellor Ken Clarke for their first four years in office. Then they let rip. From 2002 to 2010 Gordon Brown ran the economy £564.5 billion into debt. Even when the economy was booming between 2002 and 2008 under Blair and Brown the UK was still borrowing heavily. What percentage of the £41 billion Britain borrowed from abroad in 2005 or the £68 billion borrowed in 2008 was used to cover the additional costs associated with immigration we are still not allowed to know, even though it is our money, because it's a politically correct secret.

At no point during the boom years was public debt paid down to manageable levels in order to maintain public spending without having to cut public services, so when the post Lehmann Bros downturn came in 2008 Britain was already in hock up to the eyeballs with the added burden of a big additional population and rising unemployment.

What happens when Britain's dwindling resources are called upon to cope with a crisis in the NHS or schools or policing, or power cuts on a permanent basis? Suddenly the allocation of scarce resources then becomes a political nightmare that makes the 'British Jobs for British Workers' protest of 2009 look tame. New Labour, now safe in opposition, can look on from the edge of the abyss they created which they conveniently blame on the banking crisis of 2008.

That cost the UK taxpayer £73 billion to resolve temporarily, money we may never see returned unless there's a miracle rise in the stock market before the next collapse. Even that sum will turn out to be chickenfeed compared to New Labour's £multi-trillion spending black hole that will never be clawed back.

As far as immigration is concerned the penny still hasn't dropped for Ed Miliband and his colleagues.

Since 2000 over 60% of new asylum seekers have been refused permission to stay in Britain. However, very few of those who fail to be granted asylum are ever removed. The cost of deporting even one family of illegal immigrants is estimated by the UK Border Agency at between £26,000-£60,000 (3).

The National Audit Office estimates removal costs £11,000 per individual. The Institute of Public Policy Research estimates that to deport just the illegal immigrant population now living in the UK would cost more than £4.7 billion, and that estimate is based on official figures from the National Audit office which are believed to grossly underestimate the number of illegals living here.

There is still a backlog of half a million official asylum cases to be dealt with. While these economic migrants are here and not working or paying tax but still able to access the welfare state we must continue to borrow money to pay for them, that money will eventually bankrupt the economy. If we give them amnesty they will still have no work but will now be entitled to bring their wives and children over to live here legally, which will add yet more to the economic deficit.

The only possible, and short term, benefit that could accrue would be if all the economies of the West had a sudden intense and decades long spurt of economic activity that would mop up all the unemployed migrants who would then pay tax into the economy. This, as we will see, is never going to happen.

Without a return of cheap and plentiful energy globalisation is finished and we must turn to a limited form of protectionism to save our nation and our way of life.

For the leaders of post-war Europe protectionism was to blame for the rise of Hitler and free trade or globalisation was the only way to stop nationalism rising again. This was and is the default setting of the EU.

What is overlooked by the EU elite is that the stability, freedom and progress of the post war period up until 1979 was not based on globalisation but on largely protectionist policies. Neville Chamberlain, of all people, brought prosperity to Britain after the Wall Street Crash of 1929 with low interest rates, cuts in the welfare budget and yes, protectionism. In Britain, Labour's 1945 government nationalised the railways, the mines and created the NHS. It was not part of any globalised system.

Certain selective trade barriers, tariffs and quotas ensured almost full employment and social cohesion during this era.

With the election of Thatcher/Reagan came the obsession with free trade and the deregulation of the banking system which led to manufacturing industry in Britain and America being stripped out and sent lock stock and barrel overseas to be operated by cheap labour. British workers and British jobs in steel making, mining and textile production were traded in for foreign imports from low-wage economies like China.

The higher priced goods that kept Britons in jobs were no more as we made the transition to a world of McJobs, spiv banking, unemployment and mass immigration. Britain signed up to European treaties banning state intervention and insisting on the free movement of labour and as a result we have structural unemployment and the dismantling of our national borders at a time when England is the most crowded nation in Europe. Our finances are haemorrhaging and all the while there is no slowing the inrush of foreigners to our shores.

In the 2010 Conservative election manifesto David Cameron promised to bring the level of net immigration down to "tens of thousands rather than hundreds of thousands". Now in government, this has been watered down to vague promises regarding an annual limit on work permits.

Their coalition partners, the Lib-Dems, want an amnesty for illegal immigrants and offer no limits to future immigration. Without a target being set for net immigration the Westminster club faces the very real prospect of extremist parties like the BNP filling the vacuum they are leaving in the issue the British electorate are most concerned about. In a poll conducted by a national Sunday newspaper 48% of those questioned said they would support any right wing non-racist party willing to deal with immigration. (4).

If the average Brit is willing to lurch to the right it may be the left's unwillingness to deal with immigration that will be to blame. The self-censoring of debate for fear of offending the sacred cows of PC does not make the need for that debate go away, it just sends it underground. Behind closed doors, in millions of households all over Britain people are still talking about the changes they have seen with their own eyes on the streets of their towns and cities. There are no mainstream parties who address the genuine concerns of the white working-class and the danger is that this political vacuum will soon be filled by those with extremist, non-libertarian solutions.

England is twice as crowded as Germany, four times that of France and twelve times as populated as the US. How will Britain cope with such numbers and their dependents in a permanent low or no growth economy?

According to official government projections, immigration will result in a UK population increase of six million up to 2031. That's a more conservative figure than the one supplied by Frank Field's all-party group but is still six times the population of Birmingham. Immigrants and their descendants will account for 83% of future population growth in the UK and that does not include illegal immigrants.

White Britons will become a minority by 2066, according to the ONS. That shouldn't matter say those who favour multiculturalism but where is the evidence that multiculturalism has worked better than homogeneous societies anywhere else in the world?

China and India, the world's leading producers of saleable goods allow very little immigration. Another society without immigrants is Japan, supposedly in recession, but still able to export $124 billion worth of high tech manufactured goods to China in 2011. Former New Labour minister Frank Field explained: 'We cannot afford to let our population grow at the extraordinary pace now officially forecast. The pressures on our public services and communities would be too great to bear.' (5).

About 50,000 illegal entrants to the UK are detected every year. In 2009, a report by the London School of Economics commissioned by the Mayor's Office in London put the total number of illegal immigrants in Britain at 725,000 (in 2007). The study found the number of illegal immigrants nationally had risen by nearly 300,000 in six years. Previous estimates in 2001 put the number of illegal immigrants in Britain at about 430,000.

As already mentioned just the current number of legal immigrants will mean the need for about 1.5 million new houses in the period up to 2026 which will result in the concreting over of vast swathes of the English landscape.

The rumblings of discontent over allocation of resources, housing and jobs is already growing. In 2009, New Labour Immigration Minister Phil Woolas was reported to be frantically advising the electorate to vote Conservative rather than for the BNP in the upcoming European parliamentary elections. Mr Woolas was booted out of his Oldham seat in 2010 after being exposed as a liar by the electoral commission, but the damage done by his party's immigration policies were only beginning to surface. Under New Labour claiming asylum had already become an open door to a permanent stay in Britain. After three Conservative election victories rather than putting trust in a return to traditional voting patterns New Labour strategists decided instead to import a whole new sector of voters from abroad. They would be doubly beholden to a government who let them settle here in the first place and then gave them jobs for life in the public sector. Naturally, those without jobs would not want to lose their generous welfare benefits or their new homes. Hey Presto, thought New Labour strategists, no more right-wing Tory governments, ever.

Unfortunately, this scenario depended on a constantly growing economy. Gordon Brown's promise of "no more boom and bust" was exposed by the banking crash of 2008 and Britain now finds itself having to support hundreds of thousands of legal and illegal immigrants who have little chance of ever finding work in Britain again but who will fight tooth and nail to remain here.

A report from the Economic and Research Institute (ESRI) in 2009 found that after the collapse of the Irish economy in 2008: "Foreign workers didn't return home after losing their jobs. In 2008 36,000 foreign nationals lost jobs in Ireland but just 15,400 left the country." (6)

They stayed on to collect benefits at a higher rate than would have been paid out in their country of origin. The amount of money now being hoovered out of the UK welfare system by recent immigrants defies calculation. The UK Border Agency (UKBA), described as "not fit for purpose" by Labour home secretary John Reid continues to be a national joke.

Its job is supposed to be screening out illegal immigrants but those who run it seem to have little idea about who or how many people are entering Britain while former immigrants on its staff have been found to be corrupt.

One member of UKBA was a British citizen of Nigerian origin, Benjamin Orororo. He took £50,000 in bribes to grant fellow Nigerians indefinite leave to remain in Britain. Ironically Orororo, 37, of Kennington, South London, (whose wife also works for the agency), was rated a "model" officer by senior Border Agency staff at the HQ in Croydon and was featured in their in-house magazine. He was jailed for five years in October 2011.

In November 2011 it was reported that Samuel Shoyeju, an entry clearance officer, also a Nigerian, was arrested while working at the agency's head offices in Croydon. Shoyeju's high level job was to vet thousands of visa applications from Africa but he was believed to have been accepting bribes to allow Nigerians to enter Britain illegally. Scotland Yard say he will be charged with possessing false Nigerian passports and concealing substantial cash payments in a bank account in his name while either knowing or suspecting that they were the proceeds of criminal conduct. In January 2010 it was revealed that the agency had employed 11 illegal immigrants. Ten of them were Nigerians and one Ghanaian.

Should we expect any other type of behaviour from our new British citizens of Nigerian origin? In his book Culture of Corruption the author Daniel Jordan Smith found that fraud is so widespread in Nigeria that its people refer to it as "the Nigerian factor."

Smith found that most Nigerians were either willing or unwilling participants in fraud at every level of society as they try to survive in a nation riddled with corruption, vigilantes and accusations of witchcraft and cannibalism. In a land rich in oil but suffering nationwide fuel shortages Smith found Internet cafés where young Nigerians launch e-mail scams, bogus aid organizations that siphon off development money from western governments and checkpoints where drivers need to bribe police in order to proceed.

The culture of corruption found in Nigeria is possibly exceeded by that of India where 30 % of the MPs in India's parliament have a criminal record or charges pending against them. These charges range from murder to kidnapping to forgery to theft. India's school system is riddled with such forgery where fake exam certificates are available for a price and quality forged British passports are sold in Mumbai for as little as £500. The Indian legal system is a mess that would make the legal machinations described in Dickens' Bleak House look like efficiency. With over 30 million cases pending and verdicts taking decades to deliver fraud is endemic from the top of Indian society to the bottom.

Those who come to Britain from Pakistan have been nurtured in a society riddled not only with terrorism and fundamentalist religion but also corruption. A research paper by Ray Fisman of Columbia University and Edward Miguel of University of California, Berkeley called Corruption Evidence from Diplomatic Parking Tickets examined parking tickets given out to international diplomats living in New York City during 1997-2005. All foreign diplomats have immunity from prosecution in the country where they reside and so don't have to pay fines for any parking offences committed.

The authors argue that the way diplomats from different nations behave in such a situation is indicative of the cultural norms of the nations they represent.

Their results showed that Pakistani diplomats with 69.4 parking tickets each were the tenth worst offenders, behind those from Kuwait (246.2), Egypt (139.6), Chad (124.3), Sudan (119.1), Bulgaria (117.5), Mozambique (110.7), Albania (84.5), Angola (81.7) and Senegal (79.2). The results also looked at diplomats from countries with low corruption and found that those from Norway and Sweden brought the social norms or corruption "culture" of their home country with them to New York City. These diplomats had zero parking violations. Along with the financial burden to our welfare state and NHS we are importing a whole new culture of corruption from the third world where fraud and deception are a way of life.

Political correctness, an illness affecting all the major political parties in Westminster, means that pointing out the obvious could deprive you of your liberty.

In August 2011 there was no mention by any party or broadcaster of the glaringly obvious fact that the London riots took place at or near to areas with large black populations. The immediate live TV feed on the BBC news channel showed predominately blacks amongst the rioters and looters who were attacking the police in broad daylight. David Cameron said there was no racial context to the riots but from where I was sitting in front of the TV it seemed like black youths were at the very least grossly overrepresented if we consider the fact that they account for no more than three per cent of the UK population as a whole. Has Westminster been secretly invaded by Triffids from planet PC leaving our elected representatives with collective brain rot, able to mouth only "racism" at the unpalatable truth of the blindingly obvious? There were no riots in Newcastle upon Tyne, and none in Scotland.

There's no shortage of poor people in the North East as New Labour used to be aware of, so being poor was not a good enough reason for looting and rioting. What was enough reason, it appears, was being black in an area housing a large number of blacks who were also willing to riot. If saying that is construed as racist then take me away your honour. As Britain is still, for the moment, a nation of people free to speak unpalatable truths, what is also disturbing is the taboo on discussion about whether or not biology has any influence on human behaviour.

It is perfectly plausible from a scientific point of view to speculate whether biology affects the rate of development of different peoples separated by geographical distance. For those who accept Darwin's theory of evolutionary development this is an established medical fact and thus the whole concept of racism, the battle cry of multiculturalists, is almost without meaning. Yet an unholy alliance of anti-libertarian, religious and political fundamentalists are able to block legitimate scientific research on genetic differences.

In their 1994 best seller, The Bell Curve, Richard Herrnstein and Charles Murray used statistical research to show that there is a racial divide in intelligence and that the IQ of black Americans scored consistently lower than other social groups. The accusation of "scientific racism" was levelled against the authors who contended that any positive discrimination on behalf of black Americans was a waste of money, a conclusion shared by another prominent

77

geneticist Arthur Jensen of Berkeley University. James Watson, a Nobel prize-winning scientist and the genetic pioneer who unravelled DNA, reached a similar conclusion. In a visit to Britain in 2007 Watson told The Sunday Times that western economic policies towards African countries were based on the incorrect assumption that black people were as clever as their white counterparts when all scientific testing suggested that they were not. Watson was immediately threatened with investigation by the newly formed UK Commission for Human Rights and his lecture was cancelled at short notice. Any chance of a reasoned debate was over.

After the London riots police statistics showed 46 % of those arrested were black and 42 % were white. Ed Miliband made the case that the riots were the result of social deprivation and this was wholeheartedly echoed by broadcasters. They may all be right but then again, they could be wrong. Perhaps the education system needs to be reformed to meet the needs of certain ethnic groups but with only one point of view allowed and Nobel laureates excluded from debate we have no way of knowing.

What we now have in Britain is freedom of speech-lite, we can still say what we like but now only within certain proscribed areas. This madness, pioneered by New Labour and its equality legislation, has now mutated into the political criminalisation of children.

On February 20, 2012 The Yorkshire Post reported that seven-year-old Elliott Dearlove had asked a five-year-old boy at Griffin Primary School in Hull if he was "brown because he was from Africa". The younger boy's mother complained to the school which launched an investigation then phoned Elliott's mother, Hayley White, telling her that her son had been at the centre of a "racist incident".

She was summoned to the school by her son's teacher where she was read the school's zero-tolerance policy on racism and asked to sign a form saying her son had made a racist remark. Miss White, an NHS healthcare worker, refused to sign saying: "Elliott does not even know the meaning of the word racist." Since the incident she has attempted to move Elliot to a different school, without success.

"My definition of a free society is a society where it is safe to be unpopular."

- Adlai Stevenson, Detroit, 1952

Chapter Six
Police And Thieves

Watching the beginning of the riots live on BBC News 24 at 3pm on August 6, I was immediately struck that the Hackney youths running at the police, upending wheelie bins and throwing missiles had little fear or respect for the symbols of law and order.

The police in turn seemed immobilised, reluctant to do anything other than try and stand their ground in the face of naked aggression. The fear that immobilised the police was not that of being struck by the bottles or stones that rained down on them but a more abstract restraint on their response, the fear of being accused of racism.

In the topsy-turvy world of politically correct Britain the ethnic minorities squaring off to the police from eyeball distance, one sitting on a bicycle, knew they were untouchable. How did this state of affairs ever come about?

When Tony Blair expressed his sorrow over Britain's role in slavery he gave an official rubber stamp to the sense of paranoia and victimhood nursed by the Afro-Caribbean community in Britain over generations. This myth of colonial guilt for the slave trade, enthusiastically promoted by self-loathing white liberals, is now a get out of jail free card for the black community holding what they have been told is a justified grievance against British society.

This, despite the fact that we are now nine or ten generations away from British involvement in the slave trade. It's like condemning cavemen for not having good table manners. Slaving is as old as recorded human history and when England began its dalliance with the slave trade in the early 17th century Spain had already been at it for more than 100 years. Two wrongs don't make a right but West African tribal leaders and Arab slave traders had already been selling Africans into slavery for decades.

These slavers came from rival tribes who assisted white slavers in transporting other Africans to the West Indies and America where they were made to labour picking cotton or in the production of rum, tobacco and sugar.

Under New Labour the teaching of history became a non-compulsory subject in schools after the age of 14 and was then taught on the basis of topical work in thematic areas like The Tudors or American history. Any reference to the slave trade was made only as part of a more detailed study of Britain's colonial past. Subjects like the Holocaust were discarded after being deemed too controversial or too politically sensitive to Muslims. Any sense of chronology allowing children a clearer sense of what historical forces were at play moulding the actions of nations was disregarded.

Without any real knowledge of their own country's past English children were left with the message that their own culture was inferior or of less value than that of the newcomers sitting next to them in class. This is cultural relativism in action, the notion that no culture is superior or inferior to others. Cultural relativism is the battering ram of multiculturalists and the politically correct because from this point of view a religion like Islam can never be called to account or blamed for its practices. Thus traditional British culture that produced democracy, the rule of law, scientific advancement and historical figures like Isaac Newton, William Shakespeare, Thomas Paine, Charles Dickens, Charles Darwin, Isambard Kingdom Brunel....is of no greater value than the cultural norms that continue to exist in Saudi Arabia, Pakistan or Iran no matter how racist, brutal, misogynistic or homophobic. Islamic nations where sorcery and witchcraft are given more weight in law than scientific fact.

- If history had been taught in any meaningful way children might have learned that:

- Britain was the first country to abolish the slave trade. (The first French republic had tried to but their ban was overturned by Napoleon).

- After Waterloo it was Britain that insisted on spreading the abolition of slavery to other European countries.

- The Royal Navy was a major weapon used to stamp out the slave trade across the world.

- In 1833, Parliament made all slavery illegal.

There is no moral imperative in history. Bad things happen, some lessons are learned some part of humanity makes progress, some does not.

The people of Spain today are not genetically different from their ancestors who took part in the Inquisition but they no longer torture heretics. Part of the process leading to this altered state was moral and scientific enlightenment, the other was the rule of law....the shield of civilisation. On the other hand slavery has been an essential element of Muslim societies since their beginnings 14 centuries ago and remains so to this day.

The Scarman Report, commissioned after the 1981 Brixton riots argued for community policing in areas with large black populations and recommended that the police contain violence rather than actively seeking to end it by use of physical force against rioters.

Since the Scarman report police had been made to engage the black community with a softly softly approach but what really neutralised the British bobby was The Macpherson Report (1999) that followed the killing of a young Nigerian boy, Damilola Taylor, in Peckham.

Macpherson called the Metropolitan Police "institutionally racist" and made a series of recommendations which effectively crippled it as an effective deterrent to crime in London. Central to the report was Macpherson's astonishing definition of what was a racially motivated crime. He stated: "A racist incident is any incident which is perceived to be racist by the victim or any other person". So any incident can be labelled racist on the say so of, well... anybody? Was he kidding?

Apparently not, and it didn't take long for this new orthodoxy to parlay its way down to street level that rioters were untouchable in black areas.

What then followed was an unedifying scramble by the Metropolitan Police Commissioner Ian Blair followed by all the regional police forces in Britain to scramble on New Labour's PC bandwagon and with sackcloth and ashes accept the "institutionally racist" label thrust upon them and then adopt Macpherson's recommendations.

The consequences of this is watered down enforcement and large sections of London's Afro-Caribbean community coming to see themselves as beyond English law and aggressively opposed to the police, who they view as an oppressive organisation.

The widespread myth that the black community suffers disproportionally from police use of stop and search powers is countered by Metropolitan Police figures that show the following:

- About 80% of gun crime in London takes place within the black community.

- Of the remaining 20% of gun crime 75% involved at least one black person. That's black shooting white, or white shooting black. The whites involved in these shootings mostly came from Eastern Europe.

- Five times more black people (related to their proportion of the UK population) than white people are in prison in England and Wales. (Equality and Human Rights Commission's 2010 report: How Fair Is Britain?)

- Black-on-black murders are so common in London that the Metropolitan Police has created a specialist unit, Operation Trident, devoted to black-on-black gun crime.

A Home Office survey shows that up to 87% of victims in Lambeth, South London, told the police that their attackers were black. Nearly 80% of the victims were white. Black people account for 31% of the population in that area.

Under data released under the freedom of Information act in 2010 Scotland Yard statistics show black men to be responsible for more than two-thirds of shootings and more than half of robberies and street crimes in London. Based on these statistics who else should the police be stopping and searching?

On the hundred day anniversary of the London riots BBC Radio Five Live conducted a discussion with black community leaders from Tottenham. Local politicians, representatives of the police and coalition housing minister Grant Schapps were in attendance as it was broadcast on radio Five Live and the BBC 24 news channel. (1) The contributions made from the black respondents was overwhelmingly hostile to the police who were accused of being hostile to the local community. There was a general refusal to accept any responsibility for the actions of the black community during the riots and the iniquity of stop and search was constantly invoked.

The mindset of the black community, as it presented itself in this BBC broadcast, was of their hatred for the police and the belief that they are entitled to behave as they choose within their own communities. It was very depressing to hear and led to my wondering where was the way forward?

Perhaps a depoliticising of the history taught in our schools would begin to change things. Perhaps there is also an argument that politicians should stop pandering to ethnic minorities and let the police be seen to enforce the law against all those who break it, making it clear that all will be judged by the same standards.

That would mean that all of the legislation placing ethnic minorities in a de facto privileged position, like the Race Relations Act and the Race Relations (Amendment Act) 2000 would need to be repealed and the vast sums of public money that supports the race law industry and the legal shysters that feed off this legislation should be removed in order to sink the UK's multi-racial legal-aid gravy train.

"I may not agree with what you say but I will defend to the death your right to say it."
- (attributed to) Voltaire.

Chapter Seven
Our Health And Safety

We are the most crowded country in Europe but in New Labour's last year in office 591,00 more migrants were allowed to come to the UK and stay, an increase from the 567,000 allowed permanent leave to stay in 2009. And once inside Britain it appears that no one ever wants to leave.

The number of illegals deported in 2010 was 57,000, that's 15% less than the year before. As naturalist Sir David Attenborough points out, it's not about race it's about space and Britain, like the world itself, is a bounded space with finite resources.

At present Britain's finite NHS resources are being consumed by a disease that was almost extinct before 1997, HIV transmitted by heterosexual males.

In 1998 there were reported to be only147 heterosexual males with the AIDS virus in the whole of the UK, most of them infected after sexual contact with partners from overseas.

As the pace of unrestricted immigration into Britain speeded up under New Labour the UK's Health Protection Agency (HPA) found that by 2002 that figure had jumped to 3,152 with three-quarters of newly diagnosed HIV infections acquired in Africa then brought into Britain by migrating Africans. African women were by then being treated in the UK at twice the rate of African men, probably because antenatal testing had become routine in the UK.

In 2003 there was another 20% jump in the figures with the HPA recording 4,300 new cases of HIV being transmitted heterosexually, with most of these infections originating from Africa, mainly Zimbabwe. In 2004, HPA figures showed that there were between 28,000 and 30,000 Zimbabweans living in the United Kingdom, at least 10,000 of them living in London. Growing numbers of patients are now being denied treatment for conditions such as cataract operations, arthritis and cancer treatment as the NHS increasingly rations healthcare in order to save money. The Health Protection Agency reported in 2010 that 12% of the people living in Britain were born overseas, compared to eight per cent in 2001.

Research revealed that: "services for patients with mental health problems and addictions and those who need physiotherapy after accidents are being scaled back, while operations to fix hernias or remove cataracts or varicose veins are either being refused or delayed and that growing numbers of NHS walk-in centres, intended to relieve overworked GPs surgeries and A&E departments, are closing or having their opening hours cut." (1)

Primary Care Trusts (PCTs) all over England are having to reduce their service to patients as they struggle to contribute to a £20 billion savings drive.

Many PCTs are banning, restricting or imposing long waiting times on treatments that until recently were provided routinely. Beyond the cuts in services the RCN (Royal College of Nursing) has said that: "more than half of the thousands of job losses in the health service are nurses, doctors and midwives rather than managers and administrative staff."

What does it cost to look after African immigrants with HIV or an immigrant family who have three out of their six children in need of permanent medical and social care because of first cousin marriage? What is the impact on the NHS services then allotted to the rest of the population? There are no statistics available, it's a PC secret.

According to HPA statistics, in 2007 three in four of all new heterosexual cases of HIV in Britain were among African immigrants with more than 50,000 new HIV patients needing treatment in London alone up to 2010, each costing the taxpayer up to £181,000 per person. In that year, of all the cases of HIV reported in England and Wales, 25% of the diagnoses were in people of African origin, though they make up less than one per cent of the population. The contrast with diagnoses of HIV infection acquired heterosexually within the UK is astonishing. Only 275 reported in the whole of the UK in 2002 (an increase of 128 compared to 1998).

Figures released in January 2011 suggest the cost of providing HIV treatment and care in the UK could be as high as £1billion a year by 2013 if social care provision is included. A research team led by Sundhiya Mandalia

89

revealed that the UK has the fastest growing HIV epidemic in Europe with increasing numbers of patients using NHS HIV services which will: "continue to drive up population cost for HIV services," she said. Also revealed was that huge numbers of people are still being newly diagnosed with HIV each year.

From 1998 to 2002 in the UK there were 7,706 diagnoses of HIV thought to have been heterosexually acquired in Africa. The Department of Health reported in 2001 that the estimated cost of treating this one particular group, between 1998 and 2002, would be between £1.04 billion and £1.39 billion.

No one even hazards a guess at the total bill for AIDS treatment as a factor of immigration and asylum up to the present day.

Around the world 46 countries require an HIV test before admitting immigrants for any period of time. Countries like Australia, Canada and Germany from the developed world and from African nations like Nigeria, Sudan, Angola and Algeria.

Nations both rich and poor have taken precautions to protect their people and their economies from the dangers of contagious diseases. Britain, under New Labour, chose not to.

Figures produced in 2008 by the Governments own statistical service, the Office for National Statistics (ONS) showed that 605,000 people newly arrived from overseas registered with a GP in England and Wales, that's approximately one a minute, none of them were screened for contagious disease beforehand.

AIDS sufferers from abroad account for nearly all new HIV patients in Britain. As long ago as 2003 it was reported that the cost of treating HIV infected foreigners was putting hospitals into debt and threatening to halt routine operations for other patients.

Health Protection Agency figures for 2010 show that more than three-quarters of new tuberculosis cases reported in Britain that year came from people who were born overseas and that two-thirds of all newly diagnosed HIV cases and more than 80% of blood donors who were found to be carrying the hepatitis B virus were born overseas.

Dr Tim Moss, the clinical director and consultant genito-urinary physician at Doncaster Royal Infirmary, told a national daily newspaper in 2003 that politicians underestimated the problem and the huge resources needed to treat HIV patients from sub-Saharan African countries, the Far East and India.

He said that: "The situation has reached a crisis which requires central intervention. We are at saturation point. We literally cannot accommodate any more people. In the past three months we have had 10 new cases of HIV in Doncaster, six of which have been migrants. For a small town in the north of England, we are getting as many new HIV cases in three months as we would expect to get in two to three years." (2)

In the same article Dr Anne Edwards, a consultant in genito-urinary medicine with the Oxford Radcliffe NHS Trust, said: "We are now seeing a rise in local infection, which suggests that patients recently arrived in the country are having unsafe sex. We are seeing some heterosexual spread."

Dr Edwards went on to say said that some of her HIV patients were, incredibly, nurses brought over to work in the NHS from countries with AIDS problems. None of them had been tested.

Dr Edwards warned: "Our trust is in an enormous financial hole of around £20 million. Not only do we not have enough money for our own population but we are having to treat lots of people from other countries. We are shelling out huge amounts of money. A lot of people are feeling pretty resentful. Health care workers feel that some of the time we are being taken for a ride. The Government needs to come up with a system which rules on people's eligibility. If you look at all the people coming here for NHS treatment who are not eligible there are likely to be important repercussions, like the fact that your granny does not get her hip replacement. The pot of money is finite. The UK is known to be soft. It is known that if you get to the UK you can present yourself for check-up and testing."

Human rights legislation means that HIV positive visitors to Britain from third world countries are entitled to stay indefinitely while they receive NHS care.

By 2004 the potentially desperate consequences of this situation provoked The Department of Health to propose that the government exclude overseas visitors from eligibility to free NHS primary and medical services. At last a rational move in the face of fiscal recklessness, the country would be saved billions. And here's what happened. On 20 July 2009, on the last day of parliament, the Government decided: "to maintain GP discretion to determine registration to access free NHS primary care medical services along with the established principal that GPs may charge non-residents as private patients".

New Labour had blocked the move to stop health tourism costing Britain £200 million a year and in doing so continued to let anyone who managed to enter Britain by whatever means, legal or illegal, open access to primary care. A door which could lead to a much bigger door, access to secondary care.

Access to secondary care was achieved by 38 year old illegal immigrant and convicted fraudster Marshal Almansour. As reported in a national newspaper Almansour received a three year jail sentence in 2007 for defrauding banks and building societies out of more than £800,000. Now he claims he has none of it left and after an unsuccessful kidney transplant operation on the NHS he is now ensconced in a £700 per week nursing home in Stockton, courtesy of the local council, while he receives dialysis treatment three times a week. (3)

Before turning to crime Almansour's only stint of honest labour in his 14 years as an illegal immigrant was as a delivery driver and takeaway worker. Even if he'd been a nuclear scientist who'd worked for 14 years before stealing £800,000 he would still have been a gross burden on the system. That's not counting the cost of a kidney operation or the open-ended commitment taxpayers now have to his round-the-clock nursing and dialysis.

Almansour is still fighting deportation back to his native Jordan, with the aid of more public money, on the grounds that it would infringe his human rights to be returned.

Migrants are still arriving in Britain at the rate of almost half a million a year. To remove one failed asylum seeker costs the taxpayer approximately £11,000.

Factor the cost of treatment for immigrant AIDS or the added costs in more than 300 of our primary schools where over 70% of children don't speak English as a first language (that's nearly half a million children) and it's reasonably likely that even an electorate as tolerant as Britain's will demand that their representatives take drastic action when an inevitable rationing of resources deprives native British families vital services: demanding not only British jobs for British workers but British healthcare for British citizens as a right.

Political correctness rides roughshod over common sense even in matters of life and death as under European law NHS administrators are not allowed to test foreign GPs for English language skills before they begin working in NHS hospitals. If you're doing a double take right now I can understand why. In 2010 a letter from the General Medical Council (GMC) warned that some doctors on its books were unable to speak English but that under EU law this was not reason enough to stop them from working in the NHS.

They also warned that the NHS may be infiltrated by bogus doctors from other countries presenting false certificates and ID because of a lack of security checks and that they may also hide the fact they may have had their licenses to practice suspended in their home nations.

The worry was that doctors from outside Britain might not have the expertise necessary to carry out certain procedures that are standard in the NHS since there is not standardized training, education or healthcare in their country of origin.

Following this revelation was a newspaper report that foreign nurses working in the NHS and unable to speak English were failing to meet NHS standards for work on wards. Again, European Union laws barred testing foreign workers for competency in English as this conflicted with EU freedom of labour movement laws.

This abandonment of reason played out to its most bizarre conclusion with the case of Nigerian doctor Daniel Ubandi.

The GMC's letter came after the Ubani scandal where a Nigerian cosmetic surgeon was able to administer a lethal dose of painkillers to an elderly Englishman on his very first shift as a locum GP in Cambridgeshire. He was able to work as a GP in Britain without the GMC being able to find out if he'd ever even worked as a GP before! Ubandi was employed in the same year (2005) the BBC reported that 2,000 junior doctors newly graduated from medical school had failed to get a job after spending 10 years in training.

Many of these new graduates blamed competition from foreign doctors. With unemployment among young people in the UK then running at 20% the idea that we should be recruiting non-English speaking medical staff was mooted as absurd.

As foreign born nationals and health tourists continue to have free access to our NHS, without reform of the EU, or our exit from it, we have no option but to stand by and watch the service being milked of resources by foreign nationals.

MigrationWatchUK, an independent think tank believes we cannot delay if there is to be any sort of heath service left in 10 years time. Their idea is that: "Local Entitlement Offices (LEOs) should be established covering a number of Primary Care Trusts. Their staff would have specific training in administrative and immigration matters to enable them to decide on eligibility. They would also have access, perhaps by telephone, to interpreters. Once such offices were established, those who are citizens of the UK or the EU should be required to provide proof of citizenship on first registering with a GP. Other prospective patients would be given a note of the nearest Local Entitlement Office and of the documents likely to be required. The LEO's would, where appropriate, issue a Medical Health Entitlement Card (with a photograph) to those eligible. It should be possible to process such applications on the spot, or perhaps the following day if further documents were required. If necessary, there could be a fast track for those who claimed that their treatment was urgent. Visitors and immigrants could be advised when issued with their visas of the procedures necessary for access to the NHS." (4).

The problem is that even if this eminently sensible measure were adopted it would still be a case of shutting the stable door after the horse had bolted. Because of the increased cost associated with mass immigration over the next 10 years we will see the removal of the safety net the welfare state has provided its citizens since 1944. Unemployment benefit will be as rare as hen's teeth after 2015 and in the longer term will be replaced by food stamps and workfare. At almost the same pace the NHS will be transformed into a pay as you go commercial enterprise with less and less money available for free operations.

The national press reported in 2011 that Bimbo Ayelabola had travelled to Britain to give birth to quins in a blatant case of health tourism. Ayelabola, 33, had given birth to two boys and three girls by caesarean section in April, 2011 and for two weeks remained in hospital at a cost of £200,000 to the NHS. Although her visitor's visa has now expired she is fighting to remain in Britain and claims that a return to Lagos would leave her homeless and without a "support network" to help her raise her five children although it has since transpired that she has a rich businessman husband still living in Nigeria. (5)

Health tourism is not the only strain placed on the NHS by immigrants. In 2010 a survey conducted by the BBC found that in Britain more than half (55%) of all Pakistani immigrants are married to their first cousins. This inbreeding is thought to explain why a British Pakistani family is more than 13 times as likely to have children with genetic disorders. While Pakistanis are responsible for three per cent of the births in the UK, they account for 33% of children with genetic birth defects. (6)

The Danish psychologist Nicolai Sennels conducted extensive research on the problems associated with Muslim first-cousin marriages. He found that lowered intellectual capacity is the most devastating consequence of Muslim marriage patterns.

His data indicated that children of first cousin or consanguineous marriages will lose 10-16 points off their IQ with huge implications for Muslims trying to succeed in western societies. He concluded: " A lower IQ with a religion that denounces critical thinking, surely makes it harder for many Muslims to have success in our high-tech knowledge societies. The risk of having an IQ lower than 70, the official demarcation for being classified as 'retarded', increases by an astonishing 400 per cent among children of first cousin marriages."(7).

In Denmark a survey in 2007 found that two thirds of all immigrant school children with Arabic backgrounds were illiterate after 10 years in the Danish school system. The added expenditure on special education for these slow learners accounted for one third of the budget for all Danish schools. We have no similar figures for Britain because our PC political elite will not dare conduct such a survey, even when many economists and financial planners on local councils acknowledge that these are questions that must be answered in order to make future provision for those affected.

The Danish survey stated: "Those who speak Arabic with their parents have an extreme tendency to lack reading abilities - 64 per cent are illiterate ... No matter if it concerns reading abilities, mathematics or science, the pattern is the same: The bilingual (largely Muslim) immigrants' skills are exceedingly poor compared to their Danish classmates." (8)

The National Academy of Science conducted a comprehensive study into the consequences of inbreeding and found that: "The risk of having an IQ lower than 70 goes up 400 per cent from 1.2 per cent in children from normal parents to 6.2 per cent in inbred children." The study went on to list possible deleterious effects of consanguinity: "The occurrence of malignancies, congenital abnormalities, mental retardation and physical handicap was significantly higher in offspring of consanguineous than non-consanguineous marriages." (9)

The consequences of this inbreeding for British society is potentially devastating. When cousins have children together they are twice as likely to produce a disabled child. (10) The sheer numbers of handicapped children born to bigger Muslim families is infinitely greater than the number of those born to women over 40. The expense of caring for mentally and physically handicapped Muslim immigrants long term has never been calculated but calls to factor it in as a separate item of future NHS budget expenditure have been ignored.

Were New Labour politicians entirely ignorant of this situation? Surely not, as a national newspaper reported in 2008 that: "Peter Corry of St Luke's hospital in Bradford estimates that among people of Pakistani descent in the city, 55 per cent of whom marry first cousins, the risk of recessive genetic disorders – the type due to related parents – is between 10 and 15 times higher than in the general population. A 2004 study found that 13 out of 1,000 Asian children born in the Bradford area had inherited recessive disorders, which can lead to disabilities." (11).

Most states in America, Taiwan, North and South Korea and China all ban first cousin marriages. And New Labour's reaction to this ongoing tragedy? It was to allow first cousin marriage and polygamy to become part of Britain's legal framework.

Under New Labour the Department for Work and Pensions issued an order giving extra benefits for the extra wives of Muslim immigrants. It stated: "Where there is a valid polygamous marriage the claimant and one spouse will be paid the couple rate. The amount payable for each additional spouse is presently £33.65."(12).

So for every extra wife brought into the country extra benefits were paid by the taxpayer. The effects of this politically correct profligacy are now beginning to bite as the money required to cope with the offspring of consanguineous marriages has taken a large chunk out of the NHS budget as a whole. There are no official figures for this, of course, but health rationing is already upon us.

A study by the National Cancer intelligence network has found that operations to treat cancer are being rationed.

Parts of the NHS are now denying expensive surgery to remove tumours from patients who are elderly or even middle aged. Dr Mick Peake, who is based at Glenfield Hospital, Leicester, said: "There are clearly places where the teams are just looking at the patients and saying 'no'. They sit there like in the arena in the Colosseum and it's thumbs up or thumbs down." (13)

The study found that there was a severe drop in patients having cancer surgery with age and that in many cancers this started with patients in their late forties. The message to those who have paid into the system all their lives is now.... don't get old and don't get cancer, we have other priorities for NHS resources. This is just the beginning, because without economic growth the NHS is unaffordable given the service needs to provide medical cover for 3.2 million new customers and their dependents who now fill its waiting rooms. The result will be the end of the NHS by the back door.

Here's what's about to happen. It starts slowly; minor surgery.... like wart or skin tag removal that used to be free will suddenly come with a price tag, say £250. This becomes the norm and so on to the next stage where every operation comes with a price tag or conditions attached.

In his speech to staff at Ealing Hospital in May 2011 Prime Minister David Cameron warned that Britain must reduce NHS spending by £20bn over the next four years. There was no option because he had inherited that figure from the previous New Labour government.

He said: "If we stay as we are, the NHS will need £130bn a year by 2015 – meaning a potential funding gap of £20bn." (14)

In their book The Plot Against The NHS, Colin Leys and Stewart Player make clear it was the governments of Blair and Brown that began dismantling the NHS long before health secretary Andrew Lansley and David Cameron took charge.

The £101.5 billion it used to cost to fund the NHS annually was shared out amongst 150 local Primary Care Trusts, or PCTs which in turn ordered and paid for medical care from hospitals, mental health professionals and GPs on a per head basis.

For instance, in 2011 Islington in London got allocated £2268 per head of population. That system is about to be abolished to make way for the brave new world of health care where the money that once went to the PCTs will now go via a new NHS commissioning board to commissioning groups which will be professionally managed by collectives of GPs doling out billions of pounds to buy the medical care patients receive.

Soon every procedure will come with a price tag, from in-growing toenails to chemotherapy and if the money budgeted to the NHS is not enough to cover the cost of treatment then the patient/customer will have to shop around or make up the difference from his/her own savings.

All NHS hospitals will become commercial operations and able to make money from savings, and rationing. They will be able to borrow money, set up joint ventures with private companies, merge with other hospitals – and be able to go broke.

As author James Meek points out: "It was Labour that introduced foundation trusts, allowing hospital managers to borrow money and making it possible for state hospitals to go broke. It was Labour that brought in the embryonic commercial health regulator Monitor. It was Labour that introduced 'Choose and Book', obliging patients to pick from a menu of NHS and private clinics when they needed to see a consultant. It was Labour that handed over millions of pounds to private companies to run specialist clinics that would treat NHS patients in the name of reducing waiting lists for procedures like hip operations. It was Labour that brought private firms in to advise regional NHS managers in the new business of commissioning. And it was Labour that began putting a national tariff on each procedure." (15)

In 1999 the cost of the NHS was £40 billion a year, in 2011 this figure had shot up to more than £106 billion a year. If we still had the same population as we did when the service was launched in 1948 in today's terms the NHS would cost us a mere £9 billion per year. How much will it cost to fund the NHS in 5 or 10 years time?

We need to have a good look at the census figures when they eventually come out but it will be an awful lot more than £106 billion.

"A man who has nothing he is willing to fight for, nothing which he cares more about than he does about his personal safety, is a miserable creature who has no chance of being free, unless kept by the exertions of better men than himself."

- John Stuart Mill.

Chapter Eight
Cities In Flight

The changes wrought by immigration on our biggest metropolitan areas have been significant. Between the census of 1991 and that of 2001 it was reported that a "white flight" had began to gather pace in Manchester, Birmingham and Bradford. During this period Manchester lost 36,227 from a 1991 white population of 359,000, Birmingham 67,161 from a 1991 white population of 766,000 and Bradford 23,105 from a 1991 white population of 392,000.

Most alarming of all is the consequences of allowing unrestricted numbers of Muslims permanent residence in the UK. The largest Muslim group in Britain are Pakistani's and from 1991 the number of Pakistanis in Manchester increased by 48%, in Birmingham by 53% and in Bradford by 46%. The reason for these large increases has been because the fertility rates of women born in Pakistan are much higher than those of the indigenous white population.

In 1991 for the UK-born population as a whole the average birth rate was 1.8 children, in comparison with 4.8 for Pakistan-born mothers. In 2001 the corresponding rates were 1.6 and 4.7. The Bangladeshi population of Birmingham which stood at 13,300 in 1991 increased by 59% in 2001 to over 21,000.

There are now more than one million Muslims living in London, that's one in eight of the population. The census of 2011 has been collected and no doubt the results are already known, but will not be published until July 2012. Those who would question the absolute integrity of Westminster politicians might wonder why the release date is timed to coincide with the staging of the London Olympic Games.

Statistics supplied by the Labour Force Survey and the ONS in 2009 showed that the Muslim population in Britain had grown by more than 500,000 to 2.4 million in just four years. The Pew Centre, a research body with a scrupulous non-partisan reputation produced statistics that show the Muslim population in Britain at the end of 2010 was 2,869,000 of whom some 372,970 were unemployed, that's 13%, three times the rate of unemployment for any other religious group, including Christians. There are also estimated to be a further 200,000 Muslims from Pakistan living illegally in Britain according to MigrationWatchUK. British Muslims now account for 4.6% of the population.

On January 26, 2010 the Birmingham Mail using statistics obtained from Birmingham City Council, reported that 61% of all primary school children in Birmingham are now of Third World origin, with Asian pupils outnumbering white pupils for the first time.

These immigration and birth rates mean that the indigenous population of Britain will be totally overwhelmed within the next 30-50 years. At that point in time the green crescent flag of Sharia may well be flying over the Houses of Parliament. At the very least if Muslims form the voting majority will they be willing to authorise public funds for the upkeep of national monuments, Christian churches, the National Gallery (containing blasphemous artwork), scientific funding, historic arcitecture or the British Library and its heinous collection of books?

Some 150 languages are now spoken in schools in Reading, an indication of the extent to which the post-1997 non-British ethnic population is increasing exponentially.

This is the beginning of an unstoppable trend but why the complete absence of media scrutiny into the wisdom of Britain's ethnic and cultural makeover? It was because anyone who dared to offer an opinion on these changes risked being dismissed from their jobs. One of those who dared was Bradford headmaster Ray Honeywell who said, reasonably, that children should learn to speak English before coming to school. He was promptly sacked by his local authority.

Robert Kilroy-Silk was sacked by the BBC for criticising Sharia law in print. Those who towed the PC line prospered accordingly. In the case of Muslim women who came to Britain an unpalatable truth ignored by the BBC/PC bubble is that most are forcibly prevented from marrying outside their race or caste and must be paired off with a forced match from their country of origin. Young Muslim males tend to bring over partners from Pakistan and Bangladesh in arranged marriages. This increases the size of families and creates a huge change in the composition of the population of the areas they live in.

Under New Labour the welfare system has managed to subsidize single mothers with illegitimate offspring while stigmatising and depriving decent fathers of their rights to see their own children. Yet the politicians are struck dumb when confronted with the tyranny of the extended Muslim family whose Mafia-like tentacles reach across continents.

Before New Labour, Britain's primary purpose law meant that a new British citizen could only bring his wife over from Pakistan or Bangladesh if he could prove that the purpose of the marriage was not just to get round immigration laws.

Blair's New Labour abolished this rule when they came to power in 1997 and the by-product of binning this eminently sensible measure was to condemn Muslim women to the iron heel of theocratic repression exercised by Muslim men from front rooms across Newham and elsewhere in London. Thus they continued to be bartered and traded like slaves on their way to becoming baby machines used to produce male offspring.

In general Muslim men will not marry British educated Muslim women who they feel have been contaminated by the progressive and decadent ideas of the infidel. They much prefer their women to come from the villages back in Pakistan or Bangladesh, where the women speak no English and are desperate to escape a life of poverty and hard work.

The payback is that in exchange for the passive slave wife the slave wife's brother or maybe cousin is in turn promised a female relative already living in Britain. Having gone to state school in England this girl may be less than willing to marry someone she has never met but will not dare to refuse. Honour killings are common among Muslim families and even the implied threat of violence is enough to keep the semi-liberated Muslim girl in check.

Other ways of ensuring obedience is by kidnapping the reluctant female while she pays a visit to an elderly relative in their traditional village back home. Once outside the UK the unwilling bride will find her passport forcibly removed by family members then held prisoner until agreeing to the forced marriage.

In this way Muslim women are continuously recycled through British society without ever coming into contact with any progressive ideas or ever being able to assimilate British culture. Thus the bride of an arranged marriage will have the same six children she would have had had she stayed in her Bangladeshi village and will be at the mercy of the male members of her family who will ensure her life is restricted to the raising of her children within the Muslim ghettos of London, Birmingham, Manchester and Bradford.

The Muslim imams, mostly uneducated and virulent Islamists direct from the villages of Pakistan and given British citizenship en masse under New Labour will also have their way in radicalising a new generation of children with the added satisfaction of out-breeding the despised kuffar. Keeping down their women is the very source of Islamic power.

The huge translation industry that has grown with the influx of immigrants gives very little incentive for newcomers to learn English. No one has ever explained to the British people why it is necessary that Islam be

107

integrated into our system of values and many fear that British culture and the traditional way of life we have known for centuries will be completely overhauled by the Islamist group mind, unchanged by the modern world.

What is extraordinary is the collaboration of the liberal PC elite with the Islamists in keeping Muslim women in this state of near enslavement. No better illustrated than in the case of Shabina Begum, a 13 year old Muslim girl who attended a state school in Luton. The school had a dress code but allowed Muslim girls to wear scarves in order to preserve modesty; but after keeping to the school's dress code for two years Begum suddenly began turning up in a jilbab, a head to toe garment that exposes only a small slit at eye level.

It is likely she was told to do this by her brother, a member of Hizb-ut-Tahir, the Islamist organisation that seeks world domination and professes contempt for British freedoms. When the school asked her to change she refused and used the Human Rights Act to bring the case to court.

She lost the case but aided by none other than the Prime Minister's wife, Cherie Blair QC, won on appeal. A National Review article by academic Theodore Dalrymple later described the appeal decision thus: "In the long annals of judicial stupidity, there can rarely have been a more idiotic judgement than that given recently by Lord Justice Brooke of the British Court of Appeal. It reads like the suicide note not of a country alone, but of an entire civilisation." (1)

This was no victory for religious freedom, it was a huge affirmation of the rights of radical Islam to continue to oppress their womenfolk, the rubber stamping of medieval practices by a modern democracy.

Lord Justice Brooke, who heard the Begum appeal, is aware that Parliament is the supreme law making body and that judges are there only to interpret legislation passed by Parliament. Their tenure or job for life is supposed to ensure independence from political influence but under New Labour this all changed.

Before the election of New Labour in 1997 the Lord Chancellor, a political appointment, had overseen the selection of new judges. The consensus and moderation of previous administrations had traditionally ensured promotion by way of ability and independence of mind rather than political affiliation.

When Derry Irvine, one of Tony Blair's cronies, became Lord Chancellor the mould was broken: " He asked lawyers to contribute to New Labour at a fund-raising jamboree, and he appointed some judges to the bench who were more noted as New Labour sympathisers than outstanding legal brains." (2)

The Muslim Council of Britain (MCB) welcomed Lord Justice Brooke's ruling on Shabina Begum as a "victory for religious freedom", as they praise every piece of legislation that does the job of changing British society away from its secular roots to what they see as its Islamic future.

This is an unelected advisory board, funded by the taxpayer, who claim to represent 50% of British Muslims. Under New Labour they were given wide access to crucial government briefing papers and were even allowed to brief home secretary Jacqui Smith during the crisis in Gaza when Israeli armed forces boarded a boat bound for the Palestinian strip.

Its deputy-director Daud Abdullah is an Islamist radical who led the MCB boycott of Holocaust Memorial Day in

2006 and who openly called for Muslims to attack the Royal Navy if it tried to stop arms being smuggled to the terrorist organisation Hamas during the Gaza incident. It is this group that New Labour decided to trust with the responsibility of organising the reform of the imams calling for jihad and death to British people from the pulpits of British mosques.

The creation of the Imams National Advisory Board, who were to encourage moderate imams to preach moderately was left in the hands of the MCB, at taxpayers expense. What type of Islam will be preached by imams selected and advised by MCB founder Dr Kamal Helbawy, a member of the Islamist Muslim Brotherhood, whose aim is to have the whole world subjected to Islam and who is barred from entering the USA. Or advised by Dr Azzam Tamimi who told the BBC in November, 2004 that he thoroughly approved of suicide bombers and that given half a chance he'd become one himself. These are the words of that potential suicide bomber/ Muslim academic, who has taught at Kyoto university in Japan and written several books on Islam: "sacrificing myself for Palestine is a noble cause. It is the straight way to pleasing my God and I would do it if I had the opportunity."

Ken McDonald, head of the DPP (department of public prosecutions) under New Labour was a member of Cherie Blair's Matrix chambers. Of course with Cherie Blair QC and Harriet Harmon in situ as solicitor general it doesn't need a great deal of lateral thinking to make the not unreasonable assumption that the appointment of new judges was not made in a political vacuum.

Dr Dalrymple went on to say: "substantial numbers of young Muslim women are virtually enslaved in Britain; they grow up in what can only be called a totalitarian environment. I know this from what my patients have told me. They are not allowed out of the house except under escort, and sometimes not even then; they are allowed no mail or use of the telephone; they are not allowed to contradict a male member of the household, and are automatically subject to his wishes; it is regarded as quite legitimate to beat them if they disobey in the slightest. Their brothers are often quite willing to attack anyone who speaks to the woman in any informal context. They are forced to wear modes of dress that they do not wish to wear. Their schooling is quite often deliberately interrupted so that they are not infected by western ideas of personal liberty; ambitions for a career, they are kept at home as prisoners and domestic slaves." (3)

The segregation of women into Muslim ghettos means they never have the chance to choose smaller families like their more upwardly mobile Sikh and Hindu immigrant contemporaries. The Sikhs and Hindu's, not rigidly contracted to religious dogma, are able both to adopt the ways of their new homeland and seek new skills becoming valuable to the labour market. Muslims, who regard any learning not intrinsically linked to the Koran with suspicion, are left marooned in the areas where they first settled, dependant on welfare benefits.

Their distaste for the non-Muslim also precludes them from looking for work or alternative housing among non-believers so they stay put making up for their lack of intellectual or economic progress with a desire to increase their power by producing more babies. While no one would argue with the rights of any individual to be a member of any religion in a free society where does the ruling of judges, who say Muslims are exempt from the law of the

111

land on account of their faith, help any Muslim girl trying to integrate?

The suicide rate among British Asian women is four times the national average: faced with a life of captivity enforced by honour killings it is little wonder many young British Asian girls choose to take their own lives. These women know what happens when you say "no". They know what happened to Heshu Yones, aged 16, who was stabbed to death by her father Abdullah because he disapproved of her British boyfriend. They know about Tasleem Begum, aged 20, who was killed by her brother-in-law Shabir Hussain, who knocked her down in his car then reversed over her three times to make sure the job was done properly. They also know that in this case the judge accepted the plea of the killer that cultural factors had been in play and found Hussain guilty not of murder but of manslaughter and sentenced him to three years imprisonment, which means less than 18 months jail time.

In our democratic system this "jihad by stealth" is a strategy that will pay huge dividends for radical Islam in the long run. Areas in London like Newham have seen the white population fall from 58% in 1991 to 41% in 2001; demographers await the results of the 2011 census with bated breath. For Muslims, the creation of ethnic mini-states is the norm: hostile to notions of assimilation, integration and traditional British cultural values.

The speed at which militant Islam is already gaining ground in Britain was illustrated in a 2010 national newspaper article about Christian teacher Nicholas Kafouris, 52, who was forced out of his job at Bigland Green Primary School in Tower Hamlets, East London after complaining that Muslim pupils as young as eight were praising the September 11 hijackers and murderers as heroes.

"He told a tribunal that he had to leave his £30,000-a-year post because he would not tolerate the 'racist' and 'anti-Semitic' behaviour of Year 4 pupils.

The predominantly Muslim youngsters openly praised Islamic extremists in class and described the September 11 terrorists as 'heroes and martyrs'.

One pupil said: 'Don't touch me, you're a Christian' when he brushed against him.

Others said: 'We want to be Islamic bombers when we grow up' and 'The Christians and Jews are our enemies - you too because you're a Christian'." (4)

Ofsted said later that "almost all" of the 465 pupils at the school were from ethnic minorities and most do not speak English as a first language.

Under New Labour the state poured money into multiculturalism via local Labour councils and the results were catastrophic. Racial strife in areas like Bradford, Burnley and Oldham turned to open warfare and the division of these venerable cities into ethnic ghettos where the police dared not venture. New Labour made the mistake of thinking that all human beings are essentially interchangeable regardless of race or culture or education and that societies can thus be socially engineered without danger. That was their aim, the result of their meddling has been incalculable.

Many among the indigenous white population in these cities came to see themselves as being discriminated against and turned to the far right BNP. A study by the Times Educational supplement in 2003 found that these three cities were the most racially segregated in the country. This was clear to Ray Honeyford, the headmaster of Drummond Middle School in Bradford. Honeyford warned in 1985 that the promotion of multiculturalism in schools was leading to the ghettoisation of education in Bradford and the relegation of English to a secondary language. Looking back he confessed: "My philosophy at the time was a belief in integration, and a rejection of both racial prejudice and multiculturalism, which I felt from experience was dangerously divisive and contained the seeds of future conflict." (5)

For making this mild observation Honeyford found himself labelled as a racist and sacked, at the age of 51. Those in the teaching profession were his most vocal critics and only one colleague had the courage to speak up for Honeyford; that person was forced out of a job after colleagues said they: "No longer wished to work with him."

The London Oratory, where Tony and Cherie Blair's children were educated take no asylum seeker children at all. Today, more than one million children in British schools have English as their second language. Look for Honeyford's old school today and you won't find it. It's now called Iqra School, made up of 100% ethnic Asian pupils.

In 2007 the MCB published a document Towards Greater Understanding advising local authorities how to deal with Muslim pupils in our schools. In this document are a list of changes that the MCB would like imposed on British schools, they included:

Prayers: Schools should provide (1) extra "water cans or bottles" for washing before prayers (2) prayer facilities, separate ones for boys and girls. Schools should make available "a suitable external visitor, a teacher or an older pupil" to lead communal Friday prayers and give the sermon.

Toilets: Water available in water cans or bottles for cleansing purposes.

Social customs: No touching hands with members of the opposite sex, students or teachers.

Holidays: Vacation days for all on the two major Muslim holidays, the Eids. During Ramadan all children, not just Muslim ones, should celebrate "the spirit and values of Ramadan through collective worship."

Ramadan: No exams during this month and only halal meals must be eaten.

Clothing: Everyone must wear hijabs and jilbabs (a long outer garment down to the ankles). In swimming pools, Muslim children should wear modest swimwear (e.g., for girls, full leotards and leggings). Islamic amulets must be permitted.

Sports: Sex-segregation where there is physical contact with other team players, as in basketball and football, or when exposed, as in swimming.

Music: Should be limited to "the human voice and non-tuneable percussion instruments such as drums."

Dancing: No dancing allowed unless it is done in a single-sex environment and does not "involve sexual connotations and messages."

Teacher training: Staff should undergo Islamic awareness training.

Art: Muslim pupils must be exempt from producing "three dimensional figurative imagery of humans."

Religious instruction: Pictures of any prophets (including Jesus) prohibited.

Languages: Arabic should be made available to all Muslim students.

Political Islam is not the face of the majority of British Muslims at present but it may be soon, the changes outlined above would turn UK schools into quasi religious institutions. The reality of political Islam is that of relentlessly chipping away at our culture, institutions, education and free speech until a new Islamic order comes into force as the Muslim population in Britain increases.

The liberal media like to believe that imams like Qatada or Omar Bakri are little more than uneducated bigots, ramming their narrow interpretations of the Koran...Salafism or Deobundism down the throats of moderate Muslim men, women and children. That's if they have thought about it at all. It may be that these messengers of medieval Islam are the biggest danger to our way of life but will we sleep any easier in our beds just by shooting the messenger? Many observers have pointed out that to change the meaning of Islam would mean the removal of the Koran as the literal word of Allah and of Mohammed as the prophet of Allah.

Most "moderate" Muslims in Britain are probably unaware of the true meaning of the Koranic verses they recite in Arabic, it is probably this lack of complete understanding that keeps the lid on more religious extremism. However as more mosques are built and as Muslims become a larger and larger percentage of the UK population more of those who recite the verses will accept what they say as a literal word of command and act upon that word. This is the growing menace faced by all democratic European nations with increasing Muslim populations, like Britain and France.

In France the Muslim minority live in ghettos or banlieus and despite making up 10% of the population these ghettos contain nearly 100% Muslim inhabitants living under Sharia law. The police rarely enter the ghettos where there are no facilities at all for the non-Muslim, no courts, no shops and no schools other than madrassas, where only the Koran is taught. This is rapidly becoming the case in Britain where the failure to address the immigration issue is allowing extremist groups to enter the political vacuum vacated by the mainstream.

The growing support of the English Defence League (EDL) is an example. They held a demonstration of more than 4,000 EDL supporters in Luton on February 5, 2011. The day before, at a security conference in Munich, the Prime Minister David Cameron made it clear that the problem of Islamic extremism was very much on his mind. In his speech he said that a clear distinction had to be made between the religion of Islam and the ideology of Islamist extremism. In a clear reference to "jihad by stealth" Cameron said that: "non-violent extremists" who disparage democracy, oppose universal human rights and promote separatism were the problem, as they lured young Muslims onto the path of radicalism.

A Sunday newspaper reported that even this mild condemnation of state multiculturalism and British Islamism resulted in the Prime Minister being accused of supporting the EDL by Ed Miliband's shadow justice secretary Sadiq Khan. (6) The EDL demonstration passed off without trouble.

In 2004 it was reported that the French foreign minister Dominique de Villepin had ordered the deportation of an imam who had said in print that he agreed with the beating and stoning of women who broke Sharia law. Villepin ordered his deportation on the grounds that the mosque he had preached in had been used to incite violence, only to see the deportation overturned in a French court expressing serious doubt about its legality. (7)

That same year Jose Antonio Alonso, the socialist interior minister of Spain was reported to be considering the censorship of sermons given by imams in a desperate attempt to stop the spread of political Islam in his country. He told El Pais: "We need to get a legal situation in which we can control the imams in small mosques." (8)

This type of action would be difficult in Britain where the Queen is head of the church and the government. If we were to establish a register controlling the activities of radical imams would Muslims be able to claim, with justification, that we were irrationally discriminating against their religion? It would require the control and monitoring of all religions to avoid being seen as oppressive to Muslims unless the doctrines of the Church of England were to be changed resulting in the separation of church and state. England is essentially a system of theocratic democracy, a system that has persisted since the signing of Magna Carta. How can we legislate to curb what is essentially free speech without restricting the rights of others?

It would seem that in any civilised, democratic society the red line that should not be crossed is that of incitement to violence, but in Europe even that basic tenant runs into the quagmire of human rights legislation.

Germany does not have this constitutional roadblock but still struggles to deal with its imams. In an attempt to protect their liberal democracy from imam influence it was announced that the state would fund Islamic studies at three of its state universities in an effort to establish formal training for religious teaching more in tune with the mores of western society. However, the university of Muenster's attempts at enlightenment ended in chaos when Professor Sven Kalish, himself a Muslim, became the first professor of Islamic theology in Germany. Using the established academic discipline of historical critical method he questioned whether the Koran had ever been dictated to Mohammed personally by the Angel Gabriel, offering an alternative explanation that it may have been derived from other sources and came to the conclusion that the prophet Muhammed had never existed at all. He immediately received death threats and was advised by the German police to move to a more secure location.

Kalish stated that: "Most Western scientists turn down such an hypotheses out of respect for Islam or because they are afraid of the reactions of their Muslim friends or because they think it is speculative nonsense. The word "respect" sounds wonderful but it is completely inappropriate here because one really refers to the opposite. Whoever thinks that Muslims can't deal with facts puts Muslims on the same level as small children who can't think and decide for themselves and whose illusions of Santa Claus or the Easter Bunny one doesn't want to destroy." (9)

There are few other theologians who have been brave enough to apply the standard method of research to the study of Islam. Professor Kalish was sacked from his post at Munster University in 2008.

Today we do not know what is said in British mosques other than by the say-so of the MCB. We do not regulate, control or monitor them and so the hellfire imams continue to infect Muslim youth. In a poll conducted in 2006 it was found that over 40% of British Muslims want Sharia law and that 20% felt sympathy with the motives of the bombers who killed 52 commuters in London on 7/7. (10)

These imams, hot off the plane from preaching jihad in their madrassas in Pakistan were given a red carpet welcome to Britain with welfare benefits included by New Labour. Who were they? New Labour didn't know but some of them became well known to the general public. A newspaper reported that a Libyan imam, Abraham Ghait, was jailed in September, 2010 after indecently exposing himself to a 12-year-old girl in a public park. He pleaded guilty to two charges under the Sexual Offences Act. Ghait was one of 21 Libyan imams invited to Britain to preach at mosques during Ramadam. (11)

Another Muslim cleric was accused of marrying a London woman with the mental age of seven in order to live in the UK. Mohammed Anhar Ali, who is from a village in Bangladesh, was granted indefinite leave to remain in Britain after the arranged marriage. The marriage was with Bilqis Begum, 28, from Poplar, east London, a deaf mute diagnosed with schizophrenia. The bride's family ironically lambasted the Home Office for its failure to deport the cleric. Mr Ali disappeared in September 2004, having secured indefinite leave to remain in Britain in 2003. The Home Office admitted there was little they could do to have him deported.

Mohammed Hanif Khan was jailed in 2010 for the rape of a 12 year old boy. Khan had previously been honoured by Princess Anne at Buckingham Palace for his work as the first full-time Muslim cleric in the British prison service. Although the press have focused on the sexual misconduct of these clerics, two of the above were noted Koran scholars. New Labour home secretary Jacqui Smith did nothing to stop medieval versions of Islam like Salafism or Deobundism from becoming established amongst Muslim youth. She may well be remembered as the worst home secretary in the long history of that office.

Salafism, the wing of Islam also known as Wahhabism (in Saudi Arabia) believes Islam cannot be open to any interpretation at all, and must include the barbaric punishments of beheading, stoning and amputation. Exactly the same judicial system that was in operation when the prophet Mohammed was alive in the 7th century and which they hope to reintroduce across the whole world as soon as they gain power. This is radical Islam which pushes all moderation to the outer halls of the mosques and encourages any moderate imams still out there to get with the programme or else.

As we appease or surrender to Islamic demands we risk entering into the next stage, that of Dhimmitude. This is the Islamic system for governing those people it has conquered by jihad and who now must live under Sharia law as second class citizens. Those who will not convert to Islam are allowed to live only if they pay taxes (jizyah) to their Muslim overlords. There is now a debate going on in Egypt about what should be done with the 10 million (out of a population of 80 million) Coptic Christians.

Last year 23 died after a New Year bomb attack on their church in Cairo. Will they be forced into dhimmitude and made to pay taxes (jizyah) as second class citizens in an Islamic state or be made to convert to Islam? Copts are now routinely attacked in the street by Muslim mobs whipped to frenzy by their imams. Their peaceful protest from Shubra in 2011 was attacked by larger mobs but reported by the BBC as Christians against the Egyptian Army, no mention of Muslim extremists. There is no freedom of speech for the dhimmi and more than 100,000 Coptic Christians have fled Egypt since February 2011.

So what about the moderate Muslims so beloved of the liberal media? If we are pinning our hopes on British mosques producing a new generation of moderate Muslim citizens we need to look closer at what it means to be a moderate Muslim. How many of our 2,000 mosques are teaching extremism and jihad?

If writers such as Nonie Dawish are to be believed the answer is, all of them. She was born in Gaza and grew up in Cairo before renouncing her Muslim faith and moving to America. This is her view: "The term 'moderate Muslim' was created in the West. In the Muslim world there is nothing called moderate or radical Muslims or moderate or radical mosques. You are either a Muslim or not. For the term 'moderate' Muslim to be legitimate, we must have something called 'moderate Islam' vs. Islam. What the West terms as moderate Muslims are the good and peace loving Muslims who are not necessarily taking their religion very seriously and many of whom have never read about sharia. So what the West calls moderate Muslims are people who have lost the battle against the radicals in the Middle East. The radicals are terrorizing and controlling the Arab street and also Arab leaders who must conform to sharia if they want to survive in office.

"Just remember, Sadat and the Shah of Iran were considered infidels and that is why one was killed and the other pushed out of office by an Islamic revolution. Muslims who stand against offensive jihad, anti-Semitism or sharia's brutal laws, he or she will be labelled an apostate. That is why the voices of the so called moderate Muslims are not heard and are not a strong force for change and for the reform of Islam. Many so called moderate Muslims discovered that in the long run it is best to follow the saying 'if you cannot beat them, join them'." (12)

If there are moderate Muslims they have to keep their heads well down because there appears to be no moderate Islam and if there is no moderate Islam then why are we allowing more mosques to be built and facilitating imams who are preaching for our destruction? Dawish is pessimistic of any reform of Islam or of the existence of any moderate Muslims. Her view is that every Muslim is a potential fanatic who has yet to come into contact with the imam who will light his blue touch paper and set him or her off to kill the infidel.

"Islamic Law has slammed shut every door and window," she says. "any reform of Islam is punishable by death. Vigilante justice is allowed under Islamic Law under three conditions. There is no punishment for three murders in Islam 1) killing an apostate. 2) killing an adulterer. 3) killing a highway robber. By doing that Islamic law turned Muslims on the street into enforcers of Allah's Law. That is the power of the dreaded death Fatwa which a Muslim leader can issue against any Muslim in the world. They can call him or her an apostate. Such a Fatwa means that any Muslim in the world can kill that person and be considered a hero in the eyes of Sharia. Any attempt at change or reform is a crime under Islamic law whose penalty is death, even if the one who is trying to make the change is a Muslim leader."

Despite the obvious enthusiasm of the BBC and their reporters for the Arab spring revolts in North Africa and

Egypt the question Dawish would ask is; when the dust settles, how many "moderate" Muslims will be running things? The thanks Britain got for intervening on behalf of anti-Gaddafi forces threatened with being wiped out in Benghazi was the desecration of the graves of 150 British servicemen killed during the second world war. After being saved by the RAF Muslims chanting "Allah Akbar" attacked crucifixes in the Benghazi war cemetery with hammers and kicked over the gravestones of the Desert Rats.

The Enlightenment or Age of Reason which began in 1650 allowed Europe and America to cast off the superstition, repression and fear that had dominated the Medieval world. Enlightenment thinkers were able to question the rational basis of all beliefs and oppose the authority of the church and state. This led to all of the great scientific, political and social advances that we in the West now take for granted. The Sun did not revolve around the Earth because the church said so, the peasants got to vote, modern medicine replaced spells and incantations, there was equality between the sexes, race and religion.

This never happened in the Arab states of the former Ottoman Empire where foreign science was forbidden by the clerics and printed books banned for centuries. Once Muslim mathematicians building on the foundations left for them by the Greeks were able to invent algebra, but after the clerics established Sharia law the free exchange of ideas vital to scientific progress was banned. Religious calligraphy was all that Islam allowed and so the Muslim world was cut off from scientific advance and left marooned in the 7th century. Today the vast majority of Turks, seven out of 10, have never read a book.

A survey by the UN in 2003 revealed that only 330 books are translated into Arabic every year. In the last 1,200 years of Islam less than 100,000 books from the outside world have been translated. This is about the same number translated into Spanish from English in a single year. This cultural and scientific apartheid is reflected in the fact that if you exclude the peace prize (and one of its recipients was Yasser Arafat!), only four Muslims have ever won the Nobel Prize.

Professor Hans Kung, a leading theologian and author of *Islam: Past, Present and Future*, one of the most authoritative works on the subject, has argued that Islam is permanently stuck in the Middle Ages because it never had an Enlightenment, he said: "After the Reformation, Christianity had to undergo another paradigm shift, that of the Enlightenment. Judaism, after the French Revolution and Napoleon, experienced the Enlightenment first, and as a consequence, at least in Reform Judaism, it experienced also a religious reformation. Islam, however, has not undergone a serious religious reformation and so to the present day has quite special problems also with modernity and its core components, freedom of conscience and religion, human rights, tolerance, democracy."

If moderate Muslims are too scared to show their faces in Britain where the media are unwilling even to print a cartoon of Mohammed, where the Government cannot expel imams openly preaching treason and will not regulate mosques that allow hard line Islamists to teach children dark age concepts of punishment, then why should moderate Muslims stand up and be counted when the dominant culture does nothing to assist them?

The prominent Italian Professor of linguistics and left-leaning academic Raffaele Simone is mystified by the left's support for Islam. He said : "The values of Islam are, typically, the exact opposite of those that the left should

naturally support: freedom of expression, sexual equality, political and civil rights." (13)

The former mayor of London, Ken Livingstone's favourite "moderate" imam was Yusuf al-Qaradawi. Livingstone invited the leader of the Muslim Brotherhood to speak at a conference in London in 2004. This conference was funded by the Metropolitan Police and the Department for Work and Pensions, in other words, by the taxpayer. Qaradawi could well be Egypt's next Ayatollah if the Muslim Brotherhood gain power. Here's a quote from Qaradawi: 'Throughout history, Allah has imposed upon the (Jews) people who would punish them for their corruption. The last punishment was carried out by Hitler. By means of all the things he did to them – even though they exaggerated this issue – he managed to put them in their place. This was divine punishment for them. Allah willing, the next time will be at the hand of the believers.' (14)

Melanie Phillips, a British journalist and author of Londonistan, wrote of Livingstone: "The Labour Mayor of London, Ken Livingstone, has issued a remarkable dossier defending himself against savage criticism for (literally) embracing the prominent and important Islamic jurist Sheikh Yusuf Qaradawi in London last summer. Because of Qaradawi's noxious views on gays and women, not to mention his hatred of Israel and the Jews, his support for terrorism against Israel and his Muslim Brotherhood-style approach to other faiths (destroy or subjugate them), Livingstone's gesture managed to unite against himself an extraordinary coalition of protest — including some constituencies who would otherwise regard him as the leader of political correctness — including Jews, gays, Hindus, bi-and trans-sexuals, Sikhs, women's rights organisations, progressively-minded Muslims and the National Union of Students." (15). Phillips goes on to directly quote from the words of this imam.

"His sermons regularly call for Jews to be killed, along with 'crusaders' (Christians) and 'infidels' (everyone else). He is profoundly Judeophobic. He has said: "The iniquity of the Jews, as a community, is obvious and apparent". He has insisted that all Jews are responsible for Israel's actions, and on Al Jazeera's website stated: "There is no dialogue between us except by the sword and the rifle".

Although he says he disapproves of al-Qaeda terrorism Qaradawi supports the use of child suicide bombers against Israel: "The Israelis might have nuclear bombs but we have the children bomb and these human bombs must continue until liberation".

He approves of female circumcision. He supports the 'light' beating of wives by their husbands. And discussing whether both active and passive participants in homosexual practices should be either given the same punishment as for fornication or put to death, he says: "While such punishments may seem cruel, they have been suggested to maintain the purity of Islamic society and to keep it clean of perverted elements".

She then quotes from Livingstone's dossier defending himself from criticism over his meeting with the imam from various former political bedfellows like Peter Tatchall. Livingstone whines that Qaradawi is not a terrorist supporter but: "one of the Muslim scholars who has done most to combat socially regressive interpretations of Islam on issues like women's rights and relations with other religions." Livingstone then goes on to say of the cleric: "he is described as a supporter of terrorism, when, in reality he has been one of the most forthright Islamic scholars in condemning terrorism and groups like Al-Qaida and has tried to assist the French and Italian governments in securing the release of civilian hostages in Iraq." (16)

So, approval for Hitler's holocaust, child suicide bombers and permanent jihad against the West. Let's hear it for moderate Islam! Qaradawi is banned from entering the US and since 2008, the UK. Are there any moderate imams out there who would like to stand up for peaceful Islam in the face of official endorsement of this imam by the British police, politicians and the media? Thought not. Traditionally socialism, and particularly Livingstone's brand of socialism, believed religion to be the "opium of the people", to be tolerated in private but not funded by the public. If this is moderate Islam how much worse can the hardliners be?

Following the Arab rebellion in Egypt, in which the Muslim Brotherhood played almost no part, al-Qaradawi made a triumphant return to Egypt on 18 February, 2011 after being banned for more than 30 years.

In front of a massive crowd of Egyptian Muslims he gave the Friday sermon in Tahir Square in Cairo. In his speech he prayed for the conquest of the al-Aqsa Mosque, which means the conquest of Jerusalem and Israel. The Muslim Brotherhood are now in control of the new Egyptian Parliament and in Alexandria, where they have been in charge since the revolution, there has been a huge transition. All women are veiled and no longer dare to set foot on the beaches there. The bars no longer sell alcohol or play western music. While it is true that many Muslims have no time for militant Islam when it comes to expressing their preferences through the ballot box it is inevitably militant Islam that wins.

"It is important to mention that the principle of democracy defined as the majority ruling is not approved of in Islam."
> - Introducing Islam to non-Muslims by Ahmad Hussain Sakr and Hussain Khalid Al-Hussein.

Chapter Nine
A Warning From History

Sayyid Qutb was the most radical of all the Islamist thinkers of the last century. It was the words of Qutb that inspired Osama Bin Laden and the Muslim Brotherhood. Qutb produced a thirty volume commentary on the Koran called In the Shadow of the Koran. This mammoth work can almost be condensed into one sentence. Christians and Jews and their way of life are destined for hell and any Muslim who doesn't do his utmost to speed their journey by way of holy war will end up in the same place.

Islamists see life as being divided between the world of Islam (dar al-Islam) and the land of conflict or war (dar al-harb), so its either you've been conquered by us or you're at war with us. The Koran says that jihad is the duty of every

129

true Muslim and through jihad the whole world must come to live under Islamic rule or there can be no peace...ever. They believe the only true form of Islam was that practised during the time when the prophet Mohammed was alive back in the days of the Great Caliphate (Muslim empire) when the Muslim sword conquered the known world from Spain to North Africa and the Middle East, the west coast of Africa and over the Caspian Sea to India and the Philippines. Mohammed was the perfect man so whatever he did forms the template for what is permissible behaviour for Muslims even today.

The most dangerous Islamic sect, that of Salafi jihadism can be traced to the Muslim Brotherhood. They were founded in Egypt in 1928 with the goal of establishing a world Islamic state by force. Sayyid Qutb provided the ideology for this most successful group of Islamic militants, likely to be next rulers of Egypt. Deobundi is another branch of jihadic islam. You may be getting confused at this point as many of these sects are united only in their hatred of each other but what you need to bear in mind is that Salafism (or Wahhabi as it is called in Saudi Arabia and advocated by Bin Laden and his followers) and Deobundi, which is practised by the Taliban in Afghanistan, are virtually the same in practice.

The Muslim Brotherhood believes in the application of medieval punishments as laid out by Sharia law; death by stoning for women (accused of adultery) and homosexuals, amputations and mutilation as punishment for less severe crimes like theft..... this is the ideology that is now being taught in British mosques and madrassas, a call for war on western society and civilisation, direct from Osama (deceased) and the Taliban.

A Channel Four documentary broadcast on 14th February, 2011 used an undercover reporter to find out what was going on inside the secretive world of British mosques, and the results should have been a wake up call.

The Daral Uloom faith school in Birmingham was found to be teaching its pupils aged six and seven the need for full scale religious apartheid, hatred of Jews and Christians and the need to hate the society they live in. One imam was recorded telling his pupils that: "The Hindus drink the piss of a cow." Jews and Christians were referred to by the Deobundi imams as debauched persons and Christian churches "the gathering place of devils."(1)

The use of the word "kuffar" was routinely employed by all the imams featured in the documentary to refer to non-Muslims, a word which Dr Taj Hargey, an academic from the Muslim Education Centre in Oxford, said was the Muslim equivalent of the word "filth". A visiting imam advised the children that: "being in the company of a non-Muslim is worse than being with a Jew". Incredibly this school was regularly visited by government education inspectors who are required to ensure toleration and respect for other religions as part of their remit, and by Birmingham's chief constable, who all seemed to regard it as some model of Islamic moderation. The widespread ignorance about Islam and what its true intentions are was there for all to see. Another madrassa in Keithly, west Yorkshire showed imams kicking and punching children as young as five. There are more than 2,000 faith schools in Britain and more than 80 % of them teach this Taliban-style Deobundi Islam.

Madrassas can be set up in mosques or community centres across the country without being regulated. The imams teach in secret and no-one from the non-Muslim world has any idea about what goes on inside them. Plans now being drawn up by education secretary Michael Gove that could empower local communities to set up their own schools, including faith schools. Any such measure runs the risk of multiplying the influence of radical Islam and the imams who continue to spread the word of holy war against non-Muslims under our very noses.

Local communities rarely have the will to fight against new mosques as they are often established with the help of politicians in local and national government, people like Ken Livingstone. It was reported recently that the building of a supermosque next door to the new Olympic stadium in London's East End had been halted. The openly Islamic group Tablighi Jamaat, who the FBI describe as a recruiting agent for Al-Qaeda terrorists, were behind the plans. They were being supplied with money from Islamist groups overseas. It took more than 48,000 signatures on a petition presented by Newham locals to force the local council to stop the project.

Yet, despite Newham council's ruling against what would have been the biggest mosque in Europe, Tablighi Jamaat have vowed to go ahead with the planned mosque anyway. In a national newspaper The Muslim Council of Britain (MCB) criticised the council's decision, calling it: "unfounded hostility and hysteria". (2)

Without renewed vigilance from the Newham locals this mega-mosque will eventually be a feature of the London landscape because long odds are now stacked against the forces of moderation in Britain thanks to our politicised judges operating under the guiding hand of the Human Rights Commission in Europe. Is it their fear or their ignorance of Islam that allows those who wish to kill us and destroy our society a free hand ?

Abu Qatada arrived in Britain with his wife and five children by way of a fake passport. He had been sentenced in his absence to life imprisonment in Jordan on terrorist charges and was wanted on terrorism charges in the US, Algeria, Spain France, Italy and Germany. He still managed to claim asylum in Britain on the grounds of "religious persecution" and was immediately given substantial welfare payments and a large house to accommodate his family. Qatada was well known to intelligence services as Osama Bin Laden's right-hand man in Europe with links to Al-Qaeda going back to 1989.

In 1995 Qatada, from the safety of his new home in London, issued a "fatwa" to Muslims saying it was fine if you killed innocent women and children during terrorist acts so long as they were non-Muslims. His followers included the shoe-bomber Richard Reid who tried to blow up a jet carrying hundreds of innocent people travelling from Paris to Miami in 2001.

After thousands were killed in the twin towers atrocity of 9/11 police investigating the Hamburg cell of Al-Qaeda found tapes in the home of 9/11 leader of the Twin Towers atrocity Mohamed Atta made by Abu Qatada, preaching jihad.

When Qatada was arrested in 2001 on suspicion of plotting to bomb more innocent civilians at a Strasbourg Christmas market police found more than £170,000 in cash including £805 in an envelope marked "For the mujahideen in Chechnya". This large sum had been accumulated from welfare payments made over the previous eight years and it was only at this point that his payments were suspended by the Department for Work and Pensions. (It was later discovered that four of those subsequently charged with the

7/7 London bombings which killed 52 civilians had amassed more than £500,000 between them in benefits payments.)

Qatada then went on the run but was tracked down and arrested at a council house in south London in 2002 then detained in Belmarsh high-security prison. He was freed by English Law Lords in 2005 and put under a control order.

After the 7/7 bombings in London he was arrested again with a view to deporting him to Jordan but in April 2008 judges at the Court of Appeal ruled that this plan would breach his human rights and he was granted bail by an immigration tribunal and restored to welfare benefits. Since his arrival in Britain Qatada is estimated to have cost taxpayers £1.5 million in benefit payments, legal fees and prison costs. In January 2012 his lengthy appeals under the Human Rights Act (ECHR) eventually reached a climax with the verdict from European judges in a Strasbourg court that Qatada was not to be deported back to Jordan but released subject to stringent monitoring. The cost of this surveillance involving 60 police officers is £100,000 a week, around £5 million a year that must be paid by British taxpayers. It should be noted that Islam tells Muslims that they have no obligation to their host nation whatsoever and so welfare fraud, lying to the infidel (taqiyya) and other crimes are regarded as justified and normal behaviour. The Koran orders that there can only be peace after Islam rules the whole world and when that happens infidels will be allowed to live only as long as they pay Muslims "jizya", or protection money.

Why was a man like Qatada, dedicated to the destruction of our way of life and the murder of innocent people allowed to settle here in the first place? At least in his case we know how much he is costing the taxpayer, we still have no idea what percentage of the five million immigrants resident in Britain since 1997 are a drain on the public purse. The jihadis are jubilant, as essentially European judges are telling British citizens that the obligation of the state to protect its own people is of less importance than the rights of known terrorists to be given a fair trial to the standards demanded by Human Rights activists like Amnesty International or Human Rights Watch. Thus it has been established by the UK's judiciary and European judges that the safety of the general public in Britain comes second to the prospect that any known terrorist has been or might be subject to any potential risk of torture or other nasty behaviour in his own country that may include "humiliating" treatment.

The PC judges created by New Labour are the new power elite in British courts. When Muslim radical Emdadur Choudhury burned poppies on Armistice Day in front of horrified British service families and their children, his comment was: "British soldiers burn in hell". The average right thinking person would have expected his punishment to be more than the £50 fine he actually received from Senior District Judge Howard Riddle. "It's only £10 more than a parking ticket," Choudhury scoffed on hearing of the fine, after he refused to attend court.

No doubt the £50 will be paid from the £800 a month Choudhury is given in welfare benefits by the state he so despises. As reported in many of the tabloids on March 8, 2011: "He showed his contempt for Britain after yesterday's hearing by saying: 'I couldn't care less. I don't care about soldiers that died'." Choudhury burned poppies during a two-minute silence on Armistice Day but District Judge Riddle ruled that Choudhury's behaviour had to be weighed against his right to protest enshrined in the

Human Rights Act. Justice officials confirmed that £50 was
the lightest possible fine he could have been given.

Shaun Rusling, vice-chairman of the National Gulf War
Veterans and Families Association, said that every
serviceman in the country would see the sentence as
"disgusting". He said: "If we set fire to a Koran there would
be uproar and they would go after us, but because this is
Britain people just get upset. It is a futile sentence. For
them to insult those who have given their lives for freedom
is an affront. It is one law for them and one law for others,"
he said. (3)

Compare Choudhury's kid glove treatment to that of
David Jones, creator of the animated children's cartoon
series Fireman Sam. Passing through Gatwick airport Mr
Jones, a former member of the Household Cavalry, made a
light-hearted comment about the ease with which a Muslim
in front of him with her head completely covered by a hijab
had gotten through security, without having to show her
face. As reported in a national daily newspaper: "As he
placed his scarf and other belongings into a tray to pass
through the X-ray scanner, Mr Jones, 67, said to an official:
'If I was wearing this scarf over my face, I wonder what
would happen.' To his astonishment, he was stopped by
security staff on the other side of the checkpoint at Gatwick
and accused of racism after a Muslim security guard who
heard the remark said it had caused her offence." (4)

Mr Jones was then held by police and Muslim security
until forced to admit that his remarks "could have caused
offence."

It is the presence of fanatical imams like Abu Qatada
who ramp up the hatred that helps Islam erode our precious
freedom of speech and it is the failure of the political elite in

Britain to remove these clerics that fans the growing flame of jihad.

Another imam welcomed into Britain to preach hate sponsored by the welfare state was Egyptian-born Abu Hamza, christened "Hook" by the tabloid press. He was convicted of incitement to murder and racial hatred in February 2006 and sentenced to seven years in prison. In 2010 Hamza's lawyers won an appeal against government attempts to strip him of his British citizenship. It seems the former nightclub bouncer will soon be free to preach again but may not be deported, despite his convictions and the attempts made by the US to extradite him on the basis of his alleged terrorist activities.

Compare this to a documentary broadcast by the BBC about Dutch politician Geert Wilders which allowed Wilders to be portrayed as an insane right winger threatening the peace in Europe. The film offered no criticism of imam Shaykh Khalid Yasin, also featured in the film and described as "an American Muslim teacher, extremely popular among young European Muslims. He has embarked on a mission to de-radicalise them. He is also very critical of Geert Wilders". There was also no attempt to explain the wider purpose of Islamic ideology and its goals, the Grand Mufti of Jerusalem's support of Hitler and the Nazi Party during the second world war (some 20,000 Muslims fought in the Hanjar (Sword) SS Division against Tito's Yugoslav partisans) or the barbaric punishments that are part of Sharia law. Maybe the filmmakers, former Newsnight journalist Mags Gaven of RedRebel films and producer Lucy Hetherington, daughter of former Guardian editor Alastair Hetherington and partner of Newsnight regular Michael Crick, hadn't seen Channel Four's Undercover Mosque from 2007 where Shaykh Khalid Yasin claimed on film that Christian missionaries intentionally contaminated Africans with the HIV virus. Sheikh Yasin was later shown preaching that: "We [Muslims] don't need to go to the Christians or the Jews debating with them about the filth which they believe." In the same documentary Sheikh Yasin scorns the idea of women's equality, saying: "this whole delusion of the equality of women is a bunch of foolishness. There is no such thing." (5)

The BBC hatchet-job on Wilders was sloppy and missed a vital point. Wilders is on trial in Holland on five counts of inciting racial and religious hatred. His last trial in October 2010, collapsed when one of the judges was found to be biased against Wilders. As one national newspaper reported it: "one of the appeal court judges who ordered Wilders to stand trial had dinner in May with a potential witness, a Dutch expert on Islam, and that the judge had sought to convince the professor of Arabic studies why Wilders had to be prosecuted." (6)

The missing point is that should Wilders lose in court there will be chilling consequences for freedom of speech throughout Europe, and the freedom to criticise Islam. There is no absolute freedom of speech, most sensible people acknowledge that you can't shout "fire" in a crowded theatre or joke "I've got a bomb" on a jumbo jet.

Yet the very basis of our civilised society is that free speech is precious and fragile and should only be curtailed in extreme circumstances where its misuse would be likely to and intended to incite and cause physical violence. Wilders is criticising Islam on the basis that he believes it is a totalitarian and violent religion. That is his right. He is not, as far as I can see, advocating violence against Muslims.

What is happening in Holland and in Britain is that our political elites are attempting to criminalise free speech that may cause offence to Islam not because it incites to violence but on the basis that it may incite another emotion altogether, hatred. Incitement to hatred, within the context of a free society that engages in open political debate should never be a crime: all modern democratic society depends on differences of opinion being fought over with words rather than with violence.

Islam is rapidly gaining ground in the West where, by a combination of thuggish intimidation and political pressure on what they see as our weak PC elites it aims to introduce laws which will curtail our freedom to speak out against those aspects of Islam that offend common decency. If offending someone and inciting hatred is a crime then anyone and any Muslim can claim to be offended by any speech they want to suppress. How many Islamic states have free speech? The criminalization of speech or thought is the first act of a totalitarian state. Hate speech laws are there to stop any criticism of Islamic intentions. Wilders was not inciting violence, he was on trial for what he dared to think and to say.

What every person in the free world needs to fear right now is the attempt by a block of Islamic nations, led by Pakistan, to criminalise any criticism of Islam. Since 2005 and the Danish cartoon controversy this "Istanbul Process" has successfully manoeuvred within the UN to pass into international law UN Resolution 16/18 which would enshrine restrictions on the freedom of anyone to criticize Islam or Sharia. The Istanbul Process is being promoted by a block of 57 Islamic nations which form the Organization for Islamic Cooperation (OIC). One of Islam's most heinous crimes is "slander" defined in Sharia as saying:

"anything concerning a person [a Muslim] that he would dislike." In 1990, the OIC membership strategically adopted the "Cairo Declaration" which exempted all Muslim countries from compliance with the UN Universal Declaration on Human Rights and replaced it with Sharia law. This meant Muslim nations and Sharia could not be held to account by any international standard of decency while the OIC could still go full steam ahead with its attempt to muzzle free speech in Europe. This aim is now within touching distance thanks to the backing of US and European politically correct elites. The first victory for the OIC was when Secretary of State Hillary Clinton agreed to host OIC Secretary General Ekmeleddin Ihsanoglu in Washington, DC on December 2011 to discuss how the United States could help implement its agenda to render illegal all criticism of Islam under the guise of the trumped up concept "Islamophobia".

It's worth pointing out that the word "Islamophobia" is a totally invented word, made up by the International Institute of Islamic Thought (IIIT), a Muslim Brotherhood front group. The OIC adoption of this term as a catch-all trap for gullible liberals is testament to the close relationship existing between the OIC and the Brotherhood.

Incredibly, Resolution 16/18, calling for all countries to battle against "intolerance, negative stereotyping and stigmatization of … religions and faiths." was adopted by the UN Human Rights Council in April 2011. It's ironic that one of the nations demanding the adoption of this resolution, Saudi Arabia, refuses to allow Jews to enter its country, has no free press and forbids women to drive a car.

The next step in passing a global law that will stop all political parties from speaking openly about the real intentions of Islam will be when the EU plays host at the next Istanbul Process meeting in July 2012. The aim of the OIC is to quickly shut up the movements quietly gaining popularity in Europe where Islamic immigration has been a disaster for their peaceful and democratic way of life.

The movement of Resolution 16/18 into British law would mean that libertarian democrats who write or speak by way of attempting to promote open discussion on Islamic matters will end up in jail. If Resolution 16/18 had been adopted as law in 1942 one of its first victims would have the man who compared the "fanatical frenzy" of Muslims to that of "rabid dogs". That man was Winston Churchill.

However, when it comes to liberals exercising their right to free speech in a way the PC state objects to the state can act like lightening to shut them up, just the opposite of the way the PC state deals with radical imams.

One such liberal who was hastily dealt with by Holland's politically correct judiciary was Ayaan Hirsi Ali who was crudely portrayed by the BBC's Wilders documentary as just another right wing extremist. Nothing could be further from the truth. Somalian born Ali became a refugee after being circumcised against her will as a young Muslim girl and then forced into an arranged marriage. Her book, Caged Virgin is a call for the emancipation of oppressed Muslim women. After fleeing to Holland she became elected to the Dutch Parliament where she spoke up against the barbaric treatment of Muslim women and collaborated with filmmaker Theo van Gough on his film Submission, about enslaved Muslim women in Holland. Islam in English means submission and she wrote the screenplay and spoke the narration. The film caused offence and in 2004 Van Gough was murdered by an Islamist fanatic in broad daylight while riding his bike through the

141

centre of Amsterdam. The killer carved a sign on the corpse and pinned a death warrant for Ayaan Hirsi Ali to the body with the murder weapon, a long knife. This fatwa meant she had to go into hiding but her new neighbours, fearful of those who had killed Van Gough, wanted rid of her so she was evicted from her flat and the Dutch government then proceeded with plans to revoke her Dutch citizenship, which led to her resigning from the Dutch Parliament.

The author Christopher Hitchens noted: "Before being elected to parliament she worked as a translator and social worker among immigrant women who are treated as sexual chattel – or as the object of "honour killings" - by their menfolk, and she has case histories that will freeze your blood. These, however, are in some ways less depressing than the excuses made by qualified liberals for their continuation. At all costs, it seems, others must be allowed "their culture" and -what is more – must be allowed the freedom not to be offended by the smallest criticism of it. If they do feel offended their very first resort is to violence and intimidation." (7)

Ali was effectively booted out of Holland and now resides in America. Hirsi Ali is long gone from Holland and Wilders is on trial: there's a fearful symmetry in all this somewhere. After the killing of Van Gough viewers in Holland were shocked to see the jubilant reaction of young Dutch Muslims who voiced their wholehearted approval for his murder. At this point a white flight began in Holland that has been gathering pace ever since. It 2004 it was reported that Holland was experiencing a net outflow of migrants for the first time since 1945 with most of those leaving blaming religious conflict and cultural strife brought on by immigration as their reason for abandoning the land of their birth. (8)

Those commentators who argue that there are still relatively few crazed Muslims out there burning poppies on remembrance day or calling for Sharia law in the UK ignore how fragile democracy can be when faced with a group mentality. Abu Qatada cannot be removed from Britain nor can Abu Hamza. This is not an issue of race; it is irrelevant if new British citizens are white, black or yellow so long as they are loyal to the United Kingdom and to the values of our society.

That means that once they have been allowed in immigrants have a duty to the existing British population, whose money paid for the increased standard of living they inherit, and most of all to its laws. What we now see, due to the perverse promotion of multiculturalism, is a totally new phenomenon. British citizens whose first loyalty is to another country or religion.

We saw it in the Libyan liberation struggle where many of the fighters who helped overthrow the Gadaffi regime travelled to Libya from Birmingham, Manchester, Leeds and other cities in England containing a high number of Muslims. Those who follow the teachings of Islam may well appear to be peaceful but they are still part of a much wider movement that threatens all of western Europe.

As a first step we need to break the almost automatic link between people coming to Britain to work and then gaining citizenship, as Germany has done. Only then will the Government have the powers to control immigration and the necessary control over population growth. Our liberal democratic states have evolved over time to safeguard the freedoms of the individual not the group mind, we only need to look at how quickly the Weimar Republic fell to the determined group identity of National Socialism in the 1930s to be sufficiently warned.

"Those who expect to reap the blessings of freedom, must, like men, undergo the fatigue of supporting it."   **- Thomas Paine**

Chapter Ten
Europe On Its Knees

In 2002 Sweden's multicultural, tolerant, left of centre electorate and leadership were highly vocal in condemning their neighbour Denmark for sharply tightening immigration rules, and critical of the anti-Muslim statements made by leaders of the nationalist Danish People's Party. Denmark had decided to review its laws after inward migration rose by 85% from 1980 to 2001.

Sweden, on the other hand, continued to allow open door entry for migrants in the same way as the UK. Sweden's reputation as being a haven for immigrants spread far and wide. After the fall of Saddam Hussein more Iraqi refugees went to Sweden than to any other country in the West and its population increased by 1% per year. Its foreign born population now numbers 14.3% of its 9.4 million total.

In Malmo, one quarter of the population are now Muslim and Muslim demands in Sweden are routinely backed up with violence or the threat of violence. Of those serving more than five years in Swedish jails, and tolerant Sweden only dishes out those kind of sentences for murder or rape, roughly half are foreign born.

This is also the case in France, where Muslims make up 50% of those in French jails. The Muslim ghettos that have mushroomed all over Sweden are the same as those found in the rest of Europe. The women there are cloaked from head to foot, in constant fear of being harassed or molested by Islamic moral patrols, "the men in beards".

Many state schools in Sweden, Holland and Belgium serve halal meat in order not to offend Muslim sensibilities and this fear has also influenced what is taught in schools; there are no lessons on the Holocaust or the scientific theories of Charles Darwin any more.

The accusation of racism has been the first line of attack by Swedish multiculturalists who dominate their political institutions just as they do in Britain. However, the electorate in Sweden have at last begun to react with alarm at the turn of events gathering pace in their once peaceful country. The Swedish state, long considered the model of how a democratic socialist society should be run is now a nation living in fear due to unrestricted immigration and political correctness.

In 1970 Sweden was the fourth richest country in the developed world but by 1997 it had dropped away to fifteenth place and continues to fall.

During the past two decades immigration has completely altered the makeup of Sweden's cities, and put a huge strain on its welfare state. The percentage of foreign-born living in Sweden is now equivalent to the highest percentage of immigrants the United States ever had in its history and a visit to the public schools in one of its major cities, Malmo, shows almost no ethnically Swedish children in the classroom, and all the girls dressed in a veil. In 2008 rioting broke out in Malmö when Muslim youths took to the streets after a basement mosque in the district of Rosengard lost its state funding and they were forced to move. To an outside observer Rosengård appears to be all-immigrant zone and in 2008 the residents there went on the rampage and proceeded to burn down large areas of Malmö.

Today the number of per capita rape charges in Malmö is six times greater than that of Copenhagen, Denmark. Copenhagen is a larger city, but at the moment its percentage of immigrants is lower. Police statistics show one women is raped every two hours in Sweden where every type of violent crime has risen dramatically over the last 20 years.

Those who saw the newspaper pictures of Swedish girls Malin and Amanda who were assaulted, raped and then left for dead by four Somali immigrants on their way to a New Year's Eve party will never forget them. Yet the newspaper reported that "two men from Sweden, one from Finland and one from Somalia", had been responsible.

Of all the developed nations Sweden has gone furthest down the road of political correctness to the extent that the label "soft totalitarian" has been applied to the Swedish state. In Sweden the issue now of most concern to young females is: Do you still have the freedom not to be raped if you dress in the way you want in your own country?

For young Muslim males in Sweden the veil symbolises the Islamic line drawn between submissive Muslim women and blonde Swedish "whores" who deserve no respect and who are asking to be gang raped.

What needs to be clearly understood here is that in Islamic societies rape is supposedly punishable by death but in most cases there is no punishment for the rape of a non-Muslim. Even when the victim is a Muslim there are few prosecutions because under Sharia law the testimony of the girl who has been raped is not admissible in their courts. Gang rape is theoretically punishable by death but only if the victim is Muslim. Even then there needs to be at least four Muslim men who have witnessed the rape and seen the actual penetration for any case to proceed. As most Muslim women are forced to wear a burka that would be near impossible. If a Muslim woman reports that she has been raped under Sharia law she faces being executed because of her admission that she had relations with a man who was not her husband. This is a situation that exists today in the Islamic state of Iran.

In Muslim societies killing an unbeliever or "infidel" is not considered to be murder, yet such is the power of the PC state in Sweden that to voice any opposition against Muslim immigration means you are at risk of being accused of Islamophobia which in Sweden is equated with racism. No one protests because Swedish laws outlawing hate speech against racial minorities are vigorously enforced. Despite the number of gang-rapes of Swedish women by Muslim immigrants the native Swedes must be careful what they say if they do not want to end up in jail.

Malmo will be a Muslim majority city within 10 years but the response of the ruling left wing Swedish Social Democratic party (SAP) has been to surrender to the violence. In 2004 Jens Orback, Minister for Democracy, Metropolitan Affairs, Integration and Gender Equality said during a debate on Swedish radio in 2004, that: "We must be open and tolerant towards Islam and Muslims because when we become a minority, they will be so towards us." They hope.

Such is the climate of fear engendered in that city that during the 2006 football World Cup a Swedish man was killed by Muslim youths who objected to his wearing a shirt with the Swedish national flag displayed on it.

This is a government that knows indigenous Swedes will soon become a minority in their own country yet because of a decades old left of centre ideological consensus it can do nothing to stop it. But there are those who are still willing to protest.

Led by Jimmie Akesson, the Sweden Democrats won 20 parliamentary seats in the 2010 election, and the balance of power between the centre-right government and the left-wing opposition. Akesson denies allegations of racism, saying his party has nothing against immigrants as individuals. It's their large number that are a burden on the Swedish welfare state, he notes: "We haven't had the capacity to receive all those who have been let in. We haven't had the capacity to get them out into society, get them to work, to assimilate them into Swedish society," (1)

NORWAY

Norway is, in terms of GDP, one of the richest countries in the world with a per-capita income of £36,509 per person. Much of their wealth derives from North Sea oil but Norwegians have hardly spent a Krone of it, instead putting more than $350 billion into its State Petroleum fund now known as the Government Pension Fund, an investment for future generations. Health-care services are considered among the best in the world and are available to everyone, free. Working women on maternity leave get a year off at 80% pay and old Norwegians who want to escape their cold northern winters can retire free to government-run geriatric communities in Spain.

Norway never joined the EC, but in one fateful way they imitated the policies of their North Sea neighbour, Britain. Open-door immigration that saw the number of migrants into Norway incvrease by 300% between 1995 and 2010.

Furuset is a district at the eastern end of the capital Oslo where immigrants outnumber the native Norwegians. Muslim immigration has brought what many call a "rape epidemic" to the streets of Oslo. A police report in 2010 showed that 100% of rapes between strangers were committed by non -western immigrant males, 90% of their victims were native Norwegian women. The response of Norway's left-wing has been to blame the rape victims themselves and accuse anyone who suggests Islamic culture is a danger to women of being racist.

Norwegian author Hanne Herland wrote in her book Alarm! Thoughts on a Culture Crisis, that: "Norwegians fear speaking about that for fear of being called a racist." Blonde women in Norway are said to have begun dying their hair black to protect themselves when they go out, and travel only in groups. Parts of Oslo are now Muslim-only zones and subject to Sharia law. An unhealthy obsession with that situation led to a mad gunman, Anders Behring Breivik, going on the rampage and murdering innocent campers. Post-Breivik all criticism of Islam in the Norwegian media has been stifled though the underlying problem still remains.

HOLLAND

The Netherlands, like Sweden, had a reputation of being open-minded and open-doored on immigration had a wake-up call in 2002 when leading politician Pim Fortuyn spoke out against the prevailing consensus, saying Islam was "a backward culture," and that if it were legally possible he would stop all Muslim immigrants entering Holland.

Fortyn was not an extremist, he was openly gay and had distanced himself from far-right parties in Europe. He believed Muslims living in Holland did not accept Dutch society, would not assimilate and that Islam was a hostile religion to the West and its values. Fortyn was assassinated while campaigning in the 2002 Dutch election by an animal rights activist Volkeert van der Graaf, who said he was acting on behalf of Muslims. Two years later the artist Theo van Gough was brutally murdered in broad daylight on the streets of Amsterdam. Van Gough had made a film called Submission criticizing Islam's attitude towards women. His killer was a Dutch Islamist, Mohammed Bouyeri, who had been convicted of slashing a policeman's neck with a knife a short time before he killed Van Gough and had been given a 12 week prison sentence for that offence. Bouyeri had also been given taxpayers' money to have his parents' flat totally converted in line with Muslim tradition. Such was the extent of his contempt for the generosity he had found in Holland.

It has been reported that walking Dutch streets are young Moroccan women who have refused to wear the veil. Their reward is a "smiley" where the girl is cut from mouth to ear on one side of her face as punishment and a warning to other Muslim girls who dare to assimilate.

Pim Fortuyn's courage was in sharp contrast to the moral cowardice shown by New Labour politicians in Britain who contorted themselves into paralysis over their fear of being seen as racist. After the atrocity of 7/7 in 2005 where 52 innocent people were murdered by Islamic terrorists the response of home secretary Jacqui Smith was a demand that the media to stop using the phrase "Islamic terrorism" and instead substitute the more PC "anti Islamic activity". (2)

In 2006 New Labour came within a hair's breath of passing a law against incitement to religious hatred, an attempt to criminalise any criticism of Islam. Maybe Jacqui Smith's mind was distracted by the housing expenses, porn DVDs and bath plugs she was stealing from the taxpayer but rather than stand up for the values of order, fairness and liberty demanded by her position within Britain's democratic state she and other New Labour politicians seemed to be falling over themselves to usher in an orderly transition to Sharia law.

In Holland, anti-Islam politician Geert Wilders, who has denounced the Koran as a "fascist book" is now campaigning to halt Muslim immigration and in the last election doubled his vote to become the potential kingmaker of an emerging right-wing coalition. Wilders is now on trial in Amsterdam accused of inciting hatred against Muslims. On the first day of the trial, October 4, 2010, Wilders remarked: "I am sitting here as a suspect because I have spoken nothing but the truth." He told the court that "freedom of expression was on trial". Whatever the outcome Wilders' PVV Freedom Party now finds itself the third biggest in Holland after the June 2010 elections. He has agreed to prop up the new Dutch coalition government in exchange for tough new measures to stop non-western immigration. Wilders is determined to combat what he fears is the "Islamification" of Holland and Europe. He has predicted that within two generations Europe will become completely Islamicised, leaving America as "the last man standing" for western civilisation against totalitarian Islam.

In an interview Wilders said: " Islam is a totalitarian ideology. It rules every aspect of life – economics, family , law, whatever. It has religious symbols, it has a God, it has a book – but it's not a religion. It can be compared with totalitarian ideologies like Communism or fascism. There is no country where Islam is dominant where you have real democracy, a real separation of church and state. Islam is totally contrary to our values." (3)

In that interview Wilders claims he was barred from entering Britain in February 2009 after Lord Ahmed, a British peer threatened to call out 10,000 Muslim demonstrators should he be allowed to speak at Westminster.

DENMARK

In the 2001 election the voters booted out the New Labour-like Social Democrats in favour of a minority government that needed the support of the anti-immigrant Danish People's Party to pass legislation. The result was a raft of laws preventing unrestricted immigration into the country, even though it was a member of the EU.

In 2002 Denmark no longer allowed any new citizen the automatic right to bring his wife into the country to live and curtailed all migrant rights to claim welfare benefits for a period of seven years.

In 2011 a report by the Integration Ministry into the cost and benefits of immigration found that Denmark's strict immigration laws had saved the nation billions in housing and welfare payments. The report concluded Denmark has saved at least €6.7 billion over 10 years negating the need for any significant budget cuts, despite the economic downturn.

The report found that migrants from non-western countries like Africa, Asia and the Indian sub-continent who had come to live in Denmark ended up costing the state €2.3 billion, while those who had migrated from within western nations had actually contributed €295 million to the national exchequer.

"Now that we can see that it does matter who comes into the country, I have no scruples in further restricting those who one can suspect will be a burden on Denmark," Soren Pind, the Danish integration minister told the newspaper Jyllands-Posten, and added he was willing to let more people into Denmark who could make a positive contribution to the economy.

Up until May 2011 Denmark had around 320,000 immigrants in total which constituted 5.9% of the country's 5.4-million strong population. Yet this 5.9% still accounted for 40% of all Denmark's welfare budget. Britain has almost twice as many immigrants as a percentage of population but we still don't have any idea about how much of our welfare budget is spent on supporting them. Unlike Denmark, it seems we have no right to know.

On May 4, 2011 Demark voted back in the pro-immigration Social Democrat Party under its new leader Helle Thorning-Schmidt. She is the daughter-in-law of Neil and Glenys Kinnock and was described as a "classy" version of Harriet Harmon after making a speech to the Labour Party conference in 2010. Her first changes after coming to power were to abolish Denmark's Immigration Ministry and grant new work privileges for asylum seekers. Welfare benefits for immigrants have now been raised to the same level as for other Danish citizens and citizenship has been guaranteed for all children born in Denmark regardless of where their parents came from or whether or not they possess a criminal record.

The successful points system used to decide family reunification has also been abolished and there has been dramatic reductions in the cost of application fees needed for Danish citizenship coupled with eased requirements for permanent residency and naturalisation, including dual citizenship. The outgoing immigration minister, Søren Pind warned the new rules would lead to mass immigration and welfare abuse: "It's going to be open borders and open tills." he said . Denmark is now the most favoured destination of illegal immigrants crossing the Turkish border into Greece and in transit across Europe.

FRANCE

October 27, 2005 was the first day of a three-week orgy of violence in the Parisian suburbs the like of which had not been seen since 1968. This riot would soon escalate, becoming civil warlike in its intensity. It was triggered by the accidental deaths of two Muslim teenagers in Clichy-sous-Bois, a working-class area just outside the centre of Paris. The teenagers died after accidentally electrocuting themselves while trying to escape chasing police. This led to intense disorder which segued into clashes between the police and youths of Middle Eastern and North African origin.

In French jails more than 70% of the prisoners are Muslims, many from the Muslim suburbs known as the banlieues.

In 2005 the banlieus were war zones and today they remain no-go areas for non-riot police. French political correctness means that public disquiet over immigration is being ignored by both major partiers giving Marine Le Pen, new leader of the National Front a close third place in the opinion polls. A new French president will be elected in 2012 and Le Pen has promised to deal with the "biblical exodus" of refugees fleeing turmoil in Libya and North Africa. Her call to seal Europe's borders or be prepared to see hundreds of thousands of new Muslim immigrants come ashore has widespread support.

BELGIUM

Six per cent of the population of Belgium are Muslims but this will climb to over 10% in 2030. In May, 2011 the Flemish-language newspaper De Morgen conducted a survey among Muslim students in Brussels high schools and found that more than half were anti-semitic.

On December 13, 2011 in Liege, Belgium Nordine Amrani, a Muslim man with a history of weapons offences armed himself with hand grenades and an assault rifle then stood above the town square packed with Christmas shoppers. He threw three grenades into the crowd then opened fire killing five people, one an 18-month-old child. Another 122 were wounded.

There was no mention in the media that Amrani was a Muslim and the former Belgian prime minister Herman Van Rompuy, now president of the European Council, said: "There is no explanation whatsoever (for the attack)."

GERMANY

Before 2000 those children born to foreign workers living in Germany had no right to German citizenship. Since 2000, under a new citizenship law, these children were allowed citizenship only if one of their parents has been legally living in Germany for eight years. Even after the eight years no one who had committed a serious criminal offence or who was not able to financially support themselves or their families without having to rely on welfare benefits would be admitted.

Beyond this, if the applicant cannot speak the German language to a required standard they will be refused citizenship and if there are any "indications" which can legitimate the reasonable assumption that the applicant "follows or supports attempts which are directed against the German constitution", application will be denied. Since 9/11 very few Muslims have been granted German citizenship.

After the EU-expansion in May 2004 Germany, unlike Britain, opted for a seven year transition period before allowing migrants access to work in Germany, and then restricted that access allowing permanent settlement mainly for self-employed or for highly-skilled migrants. Germany is still the most stable and prosperous nation in Europe.

SPAIN

You don't see it much in the media but Spain is the European nation closest to being transformed into a quasi-Islamic state. In the past 10 years more than 1,000 mosques have been built in the once devout Catholic state of Spain. Councils under the control of Spain's socialist party are closing Christian churches and financing the construction of mega-mosques.

In Barcelona €30 million was set aside to finance a huge edifice for Muslim worshippers. This will rival the Islamic cultural centre in Madrid, currently the biggest mosque in Spain. Spain's socialist prime minister Jose Luis Rodriguez Zapatero came to power three days after the Madrid train bombings of March 11, 2004.

On that day Al-Qaeda simultaneously detonated 10 bombs on four Spanish commuter lines killing 190 people and wounding 1,800. Zapatero's first pledge on being elected on March 14, 2004 was to pull out all 1,300 Spanish troops fighting under NATO command in Iraq. Zapatero then called on the West to negotiate a truce with Islamic terrorists, on their terms. Zapatero also allowed an amnesty for illegal immigrants in Spain that would change the composition of its population beyond recognition. In 1998 only 3.2% of Spain's population was foreign born, by 2007 this had gone up to 13.4%.

As the Muslim population of Spain has increased so has the level of their demands. In Cordoba Muslims demanded that the Spanish government open the main cathedral to them. The cathedral used to be a mosque during medieval times when Spain was part of an Islamic kingdom that stretched as far as Afghanistan. Muslims hope to turn Cordoba into a "Mecca of the West" with the aid of Wahabbist Saudi Arabian money. All over Spain, not just in Barcelona and Madrid but in Grenada, Zaragoza, and Lleida Muslims are demanding the return of territories they lost during the Spanish Reconquistan in 1609. Al-Andalus is the Arabic name given to the areas of Spain once ruled by Muslims between 711 and 1492. Muslims believe that these territories still belong to them based on Islamic law that states land once occupied by Muslims must remain under Muslim domination forever.

All over Spain imams call the faithful to payer each Friday. Many mosques in Spain are allowed their own religious police who beat up those accused of not complying with religious law. Islam wants to restore past Muslim glory by re-establishing the Islamic empire across the Middle East, Europe and North Africa on the way to complete world conquest. It believes that Spain is still a Muslim state and must be retaken by Islam.

In 2010 it was widely reported in the Spanish press that a disco named La Meca had been targeted by Islamists because of its name and design. Under the threat of "a great war between Spain and the people of Islam" the disco was forced to change its name and convert its mosque-like architecture at considerable cost. In December 2009 it was reported that Salafists in Catalonia had kidnapped a woman and tried her under Sharia law for adultery. She was condemned to death but before she could be stoned she escaped and fled to the local police station.

The gathering pace of Islamic influence in Spain was demonstrated on December 5, 2011 when more than 3,000 Muslim immigrants took to the streets near Barcelona to complain about cuts in their welfare benefit payments. The size of the demo took the authorities completely by surprise but reflected the growing power of Muslim immigrants in the region of Catalonia.

Following the Arab Spring in Morocco, Spain's nearest Arab neighbour, intelligence services in Spain suspect that Morocco's new Islamic government may be attempting to incite protest in order to influence Spanish sovereign policymaking.

There have also been calls for the Spanish government to apologise for King Phillip III's expulsion of Morisco

Muslims from Spain in 1609 and to offer them Spanish citizenship by way of apology for mistakes made by ….the Spanish Inquisition. Clearly the Middle Ages are alive and kicking for Spain's newly radicalised Muslims.

GREECE

Immigration and sovereign debt has all but finished off the Greek nation state. In 2010 the EU's own border agency Frontex said that 90% of the illegal immigrants who entered Europe did so through Greece. Aside from its struggle with sovereign bankruptcy what strain can be attributed to the added costs of coping with more than 2.5 million illegal aliens in transit through its borders? Greece does not pay welfare benefits to those who have entered illegally but the accompanying street crime, drug dealing and prostitution has destroyed the peace and civility that once existed in Athens. In desperation the beleaguered government announced, on January 4, 2011, plans to build an eight mile long fence along its border with Turkey in an effort to prevent more immigrants from pouring in.

A statement released by Greek Citizen Protection Minister Christos Papoutsis said that more than 100,000 people had entered Greece illegally last year, and that: "Our society has reached its limits in taking illegal immigrants, Greece can't take it any more". (4)

This followed a broadcast on Greek television showing the Turkish coastguard helping land illegal immigrants on Greek Islands. Between 1995 and 2005 the Turkish authorities expelled more than half a million illegal immigrants from its territory and it is clear that Turkey is using this mass of desperate refugees to destabilise the Greek government and to alter its ethnic and social makeup, creating large Muslim communities inside Greek territory.

It is also clear that the Turkish government is prepared to imperil the security of its neighbour and hence the rest of the members of the EU in order to achieve its wider purpose which is an Islamification of Europe by the back door.

The most generous welfare state, universally regarded as a soft touch among the vast majority of migrants, is Britain (though Denmark is now also regarded as being a top target). In Athens the district of Plateia Amerikis has become known to locals as the "African ghetto" where many of the close to half million illegal immigrants living in Greece have congregated. This is the centre of a huge fake identity black market where passports and identity cards from the prized nations of Europe; Britain, Sweden, Holland and Denmark, can be bought from the gangs running the transit rackets.

Many of those who wait here are from African nations like Congo and Somalia and are confident of making it as far as the Eurostar terminal in France and then on to London where they will be waved through customs without a glance. Others come from Pakistan and Afghanistan and it is common knowledge that because of the shambolic Greek economic situation courts in the UK have ruled it can no longer guarantee the human rights of migrants and that as a consequence the UK is no longer allowed to deport anyone back to Greece once they've reached British territory.

Once in Britain the first port of call will be to the army of human rights shysters/lawyers who will happily make asylum applications to known illegal immigrants.

TURKEY

The next country to become a member of the EU will undoubtedly be Turkey. The continued stranglehold PC holds on EU policymakers is illustrated by politicians who say it is a good idea to allow Turkey to join the EU as a full member.

Ed Balls, who was New Labour's chief economic adviser to the Treasury from 1999 to 2004 and an active supporter of New Labour's open-door immigration policy during this period subsequently confessed that allowing unrestricted immigration from eastern Europe had: "a direct impact on the wages, terms and conditions of too many people in communities ill-prepared to deal with the reality of globalisation, including the one I represent." He went on to admit that: "The wages of British workers were forced down because the Labour government failed to restrict immigration from eastern Europe". (5)

This was at a point in time when Mr Balls felt he was in with a chance of winning the Labour leadership contest. Mr Balls, now Labour shadow chancellor, is in favour of Turkey being allowed to join the EU, a policy which has the potential to eclipse the damage already created by his party's catastrophic immigration policies during their long tenure in office.

"I support the political and economic case for EU enlargement to Turkey," he said, adding that: "it may well be prudent to place temporary restrictions of the expected influx of unskilled labour from Turkey once the barriers come down". (6)

A wise move considering Turkey's per capita income is still only 20% of the average EU member state. Mr Balls may not be aware that with a population expected to be around 100 million by 2050 Turkey would effectively be the major force within the European Parliament from the minute it was admitted. What is more worrying is that not just Balls but many of our major politicians, including Prime Minister David Cameron, now seem to be falling into line with a mad desire to allow Turkey entry into the EU. Others are not so sure. Cardinal Ratzinger, before he became Pope warned in an interview given to Le Figaro in August 2004 that allowing Turkey to join the EU would be a "grave error" given that its Islamic culture places it "in permanent contrast to Europe".

Turkey may have laws that limit the role of Islam in public life but the Islamic party that now rules Turkey has other ideas.

It was a shock when the Islamic AKP took power in Turkey in November 2002. Their leader Tayyip Erdogun is a former Islamic cleric who became mayor of Istambul in 1994 only to be removed in 1997 after reading aloud a religious poem that was deemed to incite religious hatred. A bid by the secular Turkish state to ban the AKP in 2008 and boot out Mr Erdogan on the grounds that they were trying to establish an Islamic state by stealth ended in failure. Mr Erdogan remains his country's leader and is likely to do so for a long time to come as pinion polls suggest that most Turks now identify themselves primarily as Muslims, not as Turks. "The AKP did not create this mindset: rather, it was born from it," said Erdogun. (7)

Life in Turkey has changed considerably since the AKP came to power. Growing numbers of hotels have created segregated alcohol-free Muslim-only beaches. One publication reported that: "Tarsus, a sleepy eastern Mediterranean town (and birthplace of St Paul), made headlines recently when two teenage girls were attacked by syringe-wielding assailants who sprayed their legs with an acid-like substance because their skirts were too short". (8)

The long term aim of the AKP is to transform Turkey into a Muslim republic and become a member of the EU. A slogan attributed to the AKP is that "democracy is a bus we can ride until we reach our station".

Smuggling illegals is now a huge industry in Turkey whose major metropolitan areas are controlled by crime gangs demanding up to $15,000 each for a passage from Ankara to northern Europe, with the UK, Sweden and now Denmark being the preferred destinations. This is now an industry worth in excess of $8 billion annually.

The vast majority of illegals come from Africa travelling by boat to Istanbul, Izmir and Mersin but increasingly the movements are from Arabs further to the east who come through Syria then Turkey. Would-be migrants from Pakistan, Kurdistan and Afghanistan who pass through Iran also transit through Turkey and then through Greece. Consequently the USA maintains visa restrictions with Greece because of the perceived risk of terrorists flowing through its borders. Many of these migrants are hidden away in slum accommodation, working in the Turkish tourist industry and waiting to swell the ranks of those already in ghettos at the centre of Athens or the port of Patras. Most of them with a steely determination and impatience to move toward their final destinations... Sweden, Holland, Denmark and Britain.

The research institute RIEAS estimates that there are currently more than a million illegal immigrants in transit between Turkey, Greece and the rest of Europe in complete and open breach of an agreement over illegal immigration and organised crime Greece signed with Turkey in 2005.

At the moment the fundamentalist lid is kept on the Turkish nation by the iron fist of its armed forces. The

Turks themselves continually vote for radical Islamic parties to govern them and there is little evidence that Turkish Muslims have any interest at all in the liberal values held dear by native Europeans.

The Prime Minister, David Cameron, has admitted to his "impatience" at the length of time being taken to admit Turkey to the EU. This is a game of poker with very high stakes but will we get the chance to say 'No' to Turkey at the ballot box? The game David Cameron may well be playing is that by allowing this huge new population influx, overnight increasing the Muslim population of Europe to more than 20%, he will break the back of direct rule from Brussels, thereby appeasing the right wing of his party. Yet just how could EU bureaucrats possibly control a superstate with 70 million new Turkish members?

When the French and Dutch voted 'No' in their Lisbon treaty referendums many of those subsequently polled said they voted as they did because of fears over the entry of Turkey into the EU fold. As it happened those 'No' votes counted for very little as both electorates were told to vote again until they came up with a result that Brussels could accept.

Cameron's manifesto promise of a referendum on Europe has been forgotten. The Turkish government is prepared for entry and believes there is an inevitable political momentum moving things their way. If it does the prospects of controlling Europe's borders look bleak because in March 2010 Turkey abolished visa restrictions for entry into its sovereign territory for most Middle Eastern countries, including Syria and Libya as the Turkish border became the gateway for illegal Muslim immigration into Europe from the Middle East. This means that once Turkey is part of the EU huge areas of the Middle East and their impoverished Muslim populations will have a legal right to live and work in Britain, and to claim welfare benefits.

Historically it is the Turkish army that has prevented Islam from having too much say in Turkish daily life but all that may change if the politicians running the EU have their way. They have imposed a key condition for Turkey's entry that the army is to have no more political influence in state affairs. This is fine by Mr Erdogan, as the army is now the only barrier to the Islamisation of the Turkish state. In a 2005 poll conducted by the Pew Centre 66% of Muslims said suicide bombing and violence against civilians was never justified. The same question was asked a year later and that figure, those who said no to violence against innocent civilians had gone down to 61%.

In private Erdogan as well as other Islamist leaders believe that Europe will soon be taken over anyway, they call it 'jihad by stealth', because of the significantly higher birth rates of the Muslims already living in Europe's cities. Once Turkey, a nation of more than 70 million, joins the EU that figure will increase astronomically.

When we wake up in our English cities to the wail of the muezzin calling the faithful to pray to Allah five times a day, when we look out of the window and hear the chatter of Arabic spoken by women covered by the burka from head to toe or the hostile looks of bearded men chanting "whore" at our unveiled women. When the freedom of speech we once took for granted is long gone, replaced by Sharia law enforced by fanatical thugs... by then it will be too late, we will be living as strangers in our own country and that time could be upon us much quicker than we think.

165

"A great vampire squid wrapped around the face of humanity, relentlessly jamming its blood funnel into anything that smells like money."
 - Rolling Stone magazine describes Goldman Sachs.

Chapter Eleven
Money-Go-Round

Every quarter the next round of sovereign debt payments fall due and it's only a matter of time before one of the de facto bankrupted nations: Greece, Portugal, Ireland and in the longer term Spain, announce a default or whatever name the Euro bankers decide to call it. Greece, and now Portugal are only surviving this quarterly hurdle with the aid of a well of German bail-out money.

The old adage of robbing Peter to pay Paul immediately springs to mind. Greece is insolvent, bust, bankrupt. It can't squeeze any more out of its population because they won't wear any more austerity, witness the constant strikes and civil unrest. Tax revenues haven't increased in Greece and the government fears a larger revolt could be triggered by more economic squeezing.

Greece will default on its payments, certainly before 2014, bringing down the Greek banks holding huge amounts of its sovereign debt and the French and Italian banks holding huge amounts of Greek debt. That's if the German voters haven't already rebelled at having to pour their hard earned cash into an unsustainable Greek banking system in order to give a further financial transfusion to a patient that is already dead.

Frank Schaffer, a finance expert with the German Liberal Party (FDP) is arguing that the Euro should be abolished allowing a return to the old national currencies. What is certain is that Germany will not continue doling out hard earned cash to resuscitate their deadbeat southern Mediterranean partners for much longer.

Schaffler openly opposed German chancellor Merkel's plan to give €123 billion to the notional €750 billion Brussels bail-out fund and has called for Greece to be kicked out of the EU rather than receiving further economic assistance. (1)

The locking together of different countries with different exchange rates and different interest rates into a single currency was never going to work outside the daydreams of the utopian Euro elite. Could it be that the people in the southern Mediterranean were never going to be as hard working or productive as the Germans or even the French? Greek competitiveness dropped like a stone after joining the single currency in 2001, as did that of Portugal Ireland and Spain, all by about 25%. Greece could never have joined the Euro in the first place without paying Goldman Sachs to fiddle its accounts to meet deficit targets set for all members. That fiddle completed it then sat back and sucked up the largesse doled out by their new partners.

German voters are still outraged over the €22 billion they have already been forced to hand over to Greece. The end result will be no Italian bail out when Italy cannot meet its financial obligations and if the Euro does survive it will be without the PIGS and with a smaller number of countries under the control of German bankers.

The problem is that Europe has run out of money, that is the kind of money that represents real wealth rather than the paper used by Greece, Ireland and the UK which is money that promises payment from an economy that is essentially worthless.

Unless a long shot like a Chinese rescue of sovereign debt materialises the Euro's collapse will in turn lead to the collapse of several European banks and sound the death knell of the British economy.

After Greece, Ireland is likely to be the next casualty of the Euro. Ireland's Central Statistics Office pointed out in 2011 that the nation's annual expenditure adds up to €55 billion while its revenues add up to only €35 billion. Ireland's total debt is a whopping 663% of its GDP. It is also likely that there are more than $110 billion worth of bad debts still held by Irish banks, courtesy of their mortgage bubble/property crash. This makes the Irish banking system a worthless front for EU/IMF borrowed money.

When the day comes that Ireland's voters get tired of throwing 50% of their GDP down the drain in interest payments, and it must come soon, a second wave of banking collapse will put paid to the Euro for good and do heaven knows what damage to the global system.

American banks are still hiding trillions of dollars of bad debt ripped off by the machinations of a few hundred Wall Street fraudsters walking the streets of Manhattan still miraculously uncuffed (to the great detriment of president Barak Obama and the rule of law). How was US treasury secretary Hank Poulson, formerly of Goldman Sachs, able to shanghai the US taxpayer out of more than $700 billion to cover up the mountain of mortgage fraud rackets that still lie festering away in American financial institutions? The lack of a Congressional inquiry into the shady dealings of Goldman Sachs executives like Lloyd Blankfein and Daniel Sparks remains a national disgrace.

If the Irish economy crashes Britain, as the world's biggest external debtor, will soon follow. Figures from the Bank for International Settlements show that British banks will take a hit of more than £140 billion if the Irish economy defaults. RBS, our nationalised bank, is believed to have loaned out more than £50 billion to Irish banks which have collectively attained junk status, as will RBS when the bad paper surfaces. All of these economic woes can be attributed to the unrestricted and unregulated greed of corporate bankers operating in the name of globalisation.

New Labour's Blair and Brown both shared a love of globalism, if little else. They both supported increasing free trade, free movement of labour across international borders and most damagingly of all, the internationalisation and deregulation of banking institutions.

The central tenant of globalism is the dogma that free movement of peoples across borders is a force for economic good. This is fine in theory so long as world population levels are stable rather than increasing exponentially and all the nations signed up can adequately control their borders. Without these basic disciplines in place globalisation allowed only a temporary increase in wealth for the developing world but ensured one outcome for all the

169

advanced nations of Europe, permanent mass unemployment and social unrest.

Globalism was catnip to the world's poor, free money....job or no job. The developed nations not only offered higher wages to the dispossessed of the Indian sub-continent and sub-Saharan Africa but the certain knowledge, gleaned from TV, the internet and sometimes from advertisements on the sides of buses, that even if there was no job available everyone could still live for free in a land of unlimited luxury. All that was required was to make your way to Norway, Sweden, Holland, or best of all, Britain.

This promise of a pot of gold at the end of the channel tunnel led a mass migration of people who had no skills at all appropriate to a modern economy moving en mass across Europe and past non-existent border control into the UK.

The arrival of this huge new pool of unskilled labour prompted UK employers to surgically reduce wages increasing competition for all jobs that required no training. The unions, having been emasculated by New Labour, could now do little but watch their unskilled members' wages cut to the bone. Protest was impossible for the unions, held hostage by political correctness and fear of being branded racist should they object to the new reality.

Many of the newcomers, skilled or unskilled, were found to be willing to work for low pay and live squats in the knowledge that even saving up a few thousand pounds over a couple of years would allow them to buy a house outright in their native land; especially if the money they earned was on the black economy.

Mass immigration doesn't just create competition for jobs it also creates competition for welfare services because there are more people wanting houses, school places, healthcare and welfare benefits. There are now more than three million people on the waiting list for social housing in Britain. A council house in London could be worth as much as £250,000 to a migrant with the right to buy. This situation is specifically hard on the native poor, homeless and those already reliant on benefits.

By the end of 2015 we are going to see living standards begin to crash in a most alarming way. There are only two gears on the modern economy, growth and recession, nothing in between. No cruise control. Without growth we have no money to pay for a surplus population not producing the goods.

As Europe's very own banker the City of London has, over the years, become Britain's most important generator of tax money. If we look at our capacity to manufacture saleable goods to the rest of the world the UK has been technically insolvent for more than a decade; a net importer relying on diminishing returns from our North Sea oil revenues and a banking sector controlled by the FSA (an international laughing stock designed by Ed Balls and Gordon Brown).

The debt crisis that effectively finished off the banking system and a looming energy shortage means it is certain that a long term return to growth will not take place for at least a decade, if ever again. During this period Britain's welfare state and NHS will become unaffordable and be removed by the death of a thousand stealthy cuts, no matter which political party is in power.

Keeping America afloat is the federal reserve bank printing money on behalf of the fraudulent US banking system at large. This short con cannot go on forever, not even a few more years. America's national debt is now more than $15 trillion, almost 100% of its GDP. The gamble is that this huge sum can be reduced in the future by a sustained period of economic growth, at least a decade, while the spending goes on at home. The real panic will be when free trade and the movement of goods and services like oil and food comes to a shuddering halt. Without global credit there can be no global trade; would you send your food overseas if there were no prospect of getting paid for it? The president is probably well aware of his limited options but what else can Obama do other than preserve the illusion of business as usual for as long as he can? The alternative is panic and the collapse of the global trade system.

America, with its vast resources and low population density will be able to maintain the illusion of prosperity longer than the indebted nations of Europe but in the long run the outcome will be just the same. At the end America will turn inward becoming fully isolationist as the rest of the world fights over the scraps. Then...well it could be a free for all of the most unpleasant kind.

What would allow Britain a temporary reprieve from this mayhem buying time to prepare for decades of hardship would be a swift exit from the EU. According to the taxpayers' alliance this would save us £130.6 billion a year, money we could use to rebuild our productive job creating industries behind a limited wall of protectionist measures and reduced free trade. Most importantly, this move would give Britain back control of its borders. Without it we have no alternative but to crash and burn alongside the other EU bankrupts. Such is the stranglehold that Brussels exerts over member nations not even a clear democratic vote is enough to gain release from its grasp. A simple reminder of how much the democratic process is prized in Brussels is needed.

In 2005 EU bureaucrats decided to vote themselves new powers that would put together the final pieces in the jigsaw of their planned European superstate. The Lisbon Treaty was originally a bill called the European Constitution which needed to be ratified by all EU member states in order for it to become law. Unfortunately only four of the ten planned referendums on the bill were held. The people of Luxemburg and Spain passed the bill, while the people of France and the Netherlands rejected it. As a result the referendums in Poland, Portugal, Denmark and the UK were cancelled. Rather than accept that the EU Constitution wasn't wanted by the people of Europe the EU Council repackaged it as The Lisbon Treaty, which was basically the old EU constitution under a different name, the same thing voters in France and Holland had already rejected. This time there would be no mistake, no messing around with anything as uncertain as democracy.

Despite promising British voters a referendum on the issue Tony Blair caved in to all the demands of Brussels and came back with no concessions, stitching up voters and pushing through the Lisbon Treaty as a done deal. But one stitch was dropped and a popular vote was held by one country only out of the EUs 27 nations, Ireland.

An enraged EU elite saw Irish voters reject the Lisbon Treaty by a margin of 53.4% to 46.6%. That should have been it, the treaty needed to be ratified by all 27 members, so RIP Lisbon treaty. No such luck though, Ireland had come up with the wrong answer and was asked to think again. Intense pressure was applied from the EU on behalf of the other 26 European countries (their leaders not the voters) and amid accusations of bullying and blackmail the Irish voters delivered a 'Yes' to the Lisbon treaty on 3 October, 2009 after a rerun of the original vote. Their leaders sold them out and Ireland is now owned and in hock to the European bank for generations to come.

Despite not being part of the Euro Britain has been roped into paying an initial £7 billion into the European bailout fund of €366 billion needed to rescue Ireland, Greece, Portugal then Italy and Spain. It looks like we now have no choice in the matter as the Lisbon Treaty got rid of our veto, despite David Cameron's grandstanding. Another €15 billion will be paid out by Britain in 2012 to bail out Greece and Italy via the IMF rescue fund.

In a parallel universe here's how things could have worked out had we followed Norway's example. Britain began large scale North Sea oil production in 1975, two years after we joined the European Community. Although Norway had the same amount of oil it had a much smaller population than the UK. The difference was that the UK government gave away licenses to exploit our oil wealth to oil companies without requiring any of the resultant bonanza to be used for the good of the average Brit. Norway, on the other hand, set up a state-owned corporation to ensure that Norwegians would ultimately benefit from this one-off jackpot. Britain became a net oil importer in 2006 and our population is increasing at a rate that cannot be sustained without a continuation of cheap fossil-based energy.

We have almost no manufacturing industry left and rely on the financial shenanigans of the City for most of our per capita income. What jobs we create are in retail or financial sectors with little connection to productive goods that can be traded or used.

There is but one course of action left to stop Britain moving quickly towards an impoverished or totalitarian state within the next decade.

The policy of globalism has taken millions of people out of poverty but at the cost of an out of control world population. It must be abandoned and we must re-establish some limited protection of the domestic British economy coupled with the re-establishment of border control until the massive flow of migration to the UK is ended and those living here illegally are removed.

Many jobs could be created by large rail and energy infrastructure programmes and by using the land earmarked for housing mausoleums to be turned over to food production. The already partly nationalised banking system should be required to provide finance for such undertakings. The welfare system would no longer permit enforced idleness and an increase in the minimum wage for the jobs Britons allegedly don't want to do would see tax flowing back into the national coffers.

However, creating work while we have no control of our borders would only bring about accelerated national demise by attracting an even greater influx of the world's poor. Without withdrawal from the EU Britain would not be able to re-establish control over its borders or even attempt the removal of those here illegally.

Under New Labour Britain's manufacturing base was reduced by a further 20% by exporting jobs abroad to take advantage of cheap foreign labour while our own workforce was left to rot. With an end to mass immigration British companies would be required to employ British workers rather than exploit black market foreign labour which can be laid off without employers having to fork out for severance pay.

The official jobs count says that most of the 1.7million jobs created since 1997 have been filled by immigrants and the vast majority of these jobs could have been filled by native British looking for low or unskilled work.

Government figures show that in the first quarter of 2011 one in five workers, or 20.6% of those in low-skill occupations were born outside the UK.

This figure had been one in 11 workers, or 9.0%, in the first quarter of 2002. Had these new jobs been filled by indigenous British workers (resident in the UK before 1997) UK unemployment would be officially less than 900,000 today and there would effectively be full employment in Britain. Without work, without growth, without the money to pay for our welfare services, that's when things start to get really rough. The criminalisation of legitimate protest, the neutering of the police and the coming new immigrant population explosion will bring London to a state of anarchy by the end of this decade.

By then we could see armed gangs roaming a lawless and overpopulated landscape as civilisation crumbles under mob rule and religious terror.

"A crowded society is a restrictive society; an overcrowded society becomes an authoritarian, repressive and murderous society." - Edward Abbey.

Chapter Twelve
Population/Aid Growth

The naturalist Sir David Attenborough, in a speech to the Royal Society in 2011 referred to the "strange silence" in the media when it came to discussing overpopulation. "I meet no-one who privately disagrees that population growth is a problem. So why does hardly anyone say so publicly. There seems to be some sort of bizarre taboo around the subject." He warns that on a finite planet we can halt the inexorable rise in births by way of contraception or face the consequences of: "famine and disease or war - over oil or water or oil or minerals or grazing rights or just living space." (1)

Attenborough is a patron of the Optimum Population Trust which believes that the UK cannot sustain a population level above 20 million, there are more than 61.2 million of us now living in the UK (pre-census data). This is a fact that needs to be repeated every time there are welfare cuts announced and given equal airtime with every heart tugging report of famine in Africa.

Yet strangely Attenborough, a broadcaster of impeccable liberal and humanist credentials, can't get this message across a barrier of political correctness manned by TV gatekeepers who routinely filter the debate into proscribed channels.

Carrying capacity is a term used by ecologists to describe the maximum number of animals of a given species that any given habitat can support indefinitely, without permanently degrading the environment. Many scientists believe that the human carrying capacity of the Earth is approximately 12 billion, but that figure does not take account of global warming and climate change. Modern estimates for human carrying capacity have ranged from one or two billion people living in prosperity to 33 billion people fed on minimum rations and using every available acre of land on Earth for high-intensity food production.

In 1800 there were only one billion people on planet earth. By 1930 there was double that amount, 2 billion. By 1960 that figure had doubled again to four billion. According to the UN (2010), the world's population is predicted to grow from currently 7 billion to 8.2 billion by 2030, with 1.2 billion in the developed and 7 billion in the developing world. Most of this rise in population will come from just 58 countries, of which 39 are in Africa. If the population of developing nations continues to grow at current levels the world will have to cope with 15 billion people by the end of this century.

Today, a billion people worldwide do not have access to clean supplies of drinking water. Worldwatch believes that increased scarcity of water will lead to world food shortages and this in turn to wars over water resources. There is already increasing tension between India and Pakistan over access to the Indus River, which Pakistan depends upon to irrigate huge areas of its land and which is controlled by India.

Rumour has it that accelerated industrialisation has severely depleted India's groundwater and if India were forced to build a dam to stop the flow of water from the River Indus downstream to Pakistan there would undoubtedly be war.

Without a ready supply of water for irrigation there can be no extra crops to export. America is the world's breadbasket but its obsession with the automobile means that in the short term keeping the two or three car family in petrol outweighs the need for the production of food. In 2006, US farmers distorted the world market for cereals by pulping 14 million tonnes of good quality maize (20% of its entire crop) to make ethanol, used as an alternative to petrol in motor vehicles. This took millions of hectares of land out of food production and the result was a doubling of the worldwide price of maize.

'It's a perfect storm,' Professor John Beddington, the government's chief scientific adviser, told the Sustainable Development UK conference in March 2009. He warned the audience that a combination of growing populations and food, energy and water shortages will reach crisis point by 2030. 'My main concern is what will happen internationally, there will be food and water shortages,' he said.

According to the United States Census Bureau in February 2010 there were slightly more than 6.8 billion people in the world, and this figure is growing by about 6.5

million people a month. This is just too much for the carrying capacity of the planet, Beddington warned, saying: 'If we don't address this, we can expect major destabilisation, an increase in rioting, and potentially significant problems with international migration, as people move out to avoid food and water shortages.' He added that he sees the year 2030 as the point at which things will start to fall apart badly. Beddington predicted that demand for food and energy will increase 50% by 2030, while demand for fresh water will go up by 30%. By then the world's population will have reached 8.2 billion.

Beddington warned that global food reserves are now so low, at a mere 14% of world annual consumption, that a major drought or flood could see food prices go through the roof. 'The majority of the food reserve is grain that is in transit between shipping ports,' he said. 'Added to that, the world needs to find 50% more energy and 30% more water.' (2)

Political correctness has managed to put a stop to any debate about overpopulation. If David Cameron's or any other western government wants to ring fence donations of overseas aid why should it not come with the condition of a reduction in the recipient nation's population? This would seem logical as when overpopulation was thought to be a problem of western nations in the 1970s green groups, think tanks and charities sprang up to ensure that pressure was applied to ensure populations stopped growing, which they did.

Now that overpopulation is comprehensively a problem of the developing world barely a word is uttered in favour of measures to control it. Is this because it would mean a call to reduce the numbers of brown babies rather than white?

Anyone watching the BBC's annual Red Nose day fund raising for Africa won't know that over the last 50 years western nations alone have given Africa more than £400 billion in aid, yet according to figures released by the World Bank in 2008 more than half of sub-Saharan Africans still live in extreme poverty.

The plain truth is that the vast majority of those in charge of distributing this vast wealth are corrupt and have helped themselves to most of it. This shocking fact won't ever be mentioned or discussed by the BBC because its staff are at the fulcrum of an institutionally PC state created by New Labour and fear that any exposure of that reality will lead to accusations of racism from inside and outside the corporation.

What the BBC don't point out or maybe don't know is that agricultural production in Africa is totally dependent on three factors: fossil fuels, climate and technological advances in farming and that aid does nothing to take Africans out of poverty.

In his book Dissent on Development (1971) the world's leading developmental economist Peter Bauer said there would be no Third World poverty at all if not for the intervention of foreign aid.

Because aid is funnelled through governments before it gets to the people and because, in economic parlance, rational actors always move firstly in their own self-interest, aid goes directly into the hands of corrupt government officials rather than towards emerging business or start-ups. NGO's and interest groups linked to the aid industry will fight for a share of this money rather than engaging in any productive activity that might pull their respective nations out of poverty.

We shovel money into Africa because of our liberal post-colonial guilt, says Lord Bauer, who believes the multiculturalist notion that African nations are poor because countries like Britain exploited them in the past is ridiculous. Bauer says most African nations are better off now than they were before colonialism.

Foreign aid has proved itself to be "an excellent method for transferring money from poor people in rich countries to rich people in poor countries," said Bauer.

Britain's aid programme is now ring fenced at a time when other public spending departments are facing severe cutbacks and the money we hand over to foreign countries is actually money we have borrowed, further increasing our own national debt. This is money taken from the taxpayer and given away without the taxpayer having any say in the matter. Heinous and absurd as that is the British people go on being milked without knowing why or where or in what amounts their money is being squandered.

Can someone answer this simple question? If democracy in Britain still has any legitimacy why is the government taking away the money of its own people via taxation to give away to foreigners when the country is effectively broke?

Britain alone gives the European Union aid programme more than £1.4 billion each year. Where does the money go to?

Again, according to the European Court of Auditors, it goes into the pockets of corrupt aid workers and African dictators.

For instance, examine just one recipient of Britain's ring fenced £7.7 billion overseas aid budget, Uganda. Of the

£407 million given directly to Uganda £164 million is funnelled straight into government coffers in Kampala. Uganda's de facto dictator Yoweri Museveni has been in power for 25 years and has been accused of using government money to pay for campaign bribes. He has recently bought himself a G550 Gulfstream jet to go with his collection of other jets which he uses to ferry his family to and fro between European capitals. He has also just built himself a new official residence at the cost of more than £100 million. All this while the population of Uganda live in dire poverty. (3)

British taxpayers have also donated more than £1 billion to the southern African state of Malawi over the past 15 years. Most of this cash is deposited directly into the vaults of Malawi president Bingu wa Mutharika without any questions asked about how it is going to be spent. In 2010 the amount paid in was £74 million.

That year president Bingu bought himself an executive jet and more than a dozen brand new Mercedes-Benz cars for various members of his government and had a 58-room private palace built. A British newspaper reported that: "last year his [Mutharika's] wedding to Callista Chapola, his tourism minister, cost £2 million in one of the most lavish celebrations in recent African history. The 3,500 guests at a banquet at the state house feasted on food imported from South Africa and France, and drank fine wine and champagne. The couple travelled in a white Chrysler stretch limousine flown in from South Africa and the evening ended in an extravagant fireworks display." (4) It sounds like a scene from pre-revolutionary France.

More than half of the population of Malawi, some 13 million people, live below the poverty line, many of them are starving and 16% of them have the HIV virus.

Zambian-born economist and author, Dambisa Moyo believes that the trillion dollars of aid thrown at African over the years has been a colossal waste. In her book Dead Aid, she points out that as of 2009 and despite its wealth of natural resources, the whole of the African continent accounted for just one per cent of world trade and a third of the world's poor are to be found there. Instead of talk about writing off the debts of third world nations what the West should be doing is tracking down the stolen aid money locked away in western banks by corrupt dictators and sequestering it on behalf of the people it was stolen from. Debt ridden states could then default to get a fresh start and the stolen cash used to offset or defray their accumulated debts.

As Dead Aid shows, the population of any country in receipt of international aid experiences a surge in the birth rate because aid money allows more people to survive by artificially adjusting infant mortality rates. This in turn creates even more demand for aid money because the country cannot feed the extra mouths and the population increases again. What agencies like Oxfam and supranational organisations like the EU and the UN are doing is creating a surge in the level of population in the Third World which the Third World cannot support. The meddling of the UN in politics has been incredibly destructive for an organisation whose original remit was to settle disputes among member states, period.

To complete this circle of hell as the economies of western industrial nations collapse aid will stop and the market for food and raw materials will dry up, resulting in famine, civil unrest and mass migration with the traditional farming structures which had supported a population that was sustainable relative to the environment having already been destroyed by aid subsidies. The most successful of the poorer countries in Africa are the ones that trade most with richer countries.

A 2009 interview with an English newspaper revealed: "Dambisa believes aid has stifled economic growth, bred corruption, and turned governments into lazy, unimaginative spongers. New loans to repay old have created a continent-wide state of aid-dependency. And the fact that the conditions on these loans (often of questionable value except to the donor nation) are rarely enforced has led to the de facto bank-rolling of tyrants: as late as 2006, Robert Mugabe was receiving $300m in foreign aid." (5)

The EU and the UN who finance a vast army of NGO workers whose livelihoods depend on the continued flow of aid cash would claim that it is protectionism coming from western nations that keeps the Third World in poverty.

What self loathing liberals ignore is the fact that African rulers and elites could simply refuse to trade with the West if they wanted. If they believed they were being exploited they could quickly opt to protect their own markets and develop a stronger domestic economy, the most certain way any country has to establish economic prosperity. That they don't is testament to the irresistible lure of western aid riches.

We have no vote in Britain about how much of our money is sent overseas by politicians wishing to parade their consciences on the international stage but if we stopped all foreign aid and said that those who wish to subsidise foreign nations directly can do so by giving money to private charities we would soon see how much the British public would willingly hand over. Those who have a vested interest in the continuation of the aid racket know that this sum would be a fraction of the amount currently dispersed and will fight tooth and nail to keep state-enforced aid as part of government policy.

"We are not good at recognizing distant threats even
if their probability is 100%. Society ignoring [peak
oil] is like the people of Pompeii ignoring the
rumblings below Vesuvius."
  - James Schlesinger, former US Energy Secretary.

Chapter Thirteen
The Energy Crunch Of 2015

Here's an inconvenient truth for Al Gore and the IPCC; global warming only exists in the first place because of the astronomical growth in the populations of developing world nations and the increased consumption of the developed world..... and it's too late to do anything about it.

Any change in climate will go in tandem with the availability of cheap oil and not much time remains before easily extracted oil runs out completely, maybe another 30 years. Climate change is the least of our worries.

What most geologists and now even the politicians are agreed on is that world oil production has already peaked.

In January, 2011 a report from a British all-party parliamentary group of MPs produced a report which concluded that world oil production was already passed its peak, the same conclusion reached by M. King. Hubbert decades earlier (see Appendix1). The report acknowledged that an energy crisis is on its way: "We are running into danger. Energy shortages will occur. We do not know when but the event is undoubted and it is not far distant." said the authors.

In February 2011 the International Energy Agency (IEA) factoring in current oil prices of $105 per barrel estimated that global demand would reach 90 million barrels per day (BPD) by the end of 2011(this date may be put back by a couple of years because demand has been dampened down because of the banking crisis and economic recession). The Energy Information Administration (EIA) report of 2009 predicted that world demand for oil would increase by 37% (from 2006 levels) up to 2030.

That's a jump from 86 million barrels a day to 118 million barrels a day. In its energy outlook released in January, 2011 the energy giant BP predicted that oil demand would be over 100 million barrels per day by 2030, at 102m. The problem is that the world's geological experts don't believe that the Earth can ever produce any more than 100 million barrels a day (see Ian Fell Q&A).

Despite the current price of oil at $115 a barrel oil production has remained stuck at around 85 million barrels a day for the last five years, suggesting that the industry may have the financial incentive to discover new oil fields but that there are no big oil fields left to discover.

The worry now is that oil rich states like Saudi Arabia will begin hoarding the last reserves of oil they have left in the ground for use in their own countries. This will in turn drive up the price and lead to a series of economic crashes, then small recoveries, until the world economy grinds to a permanent halt.

When we see the first major global industry collapse completely because of high oil prices we will know that despite any government assurances given, the full-blown energy crisis is upon us. The first to go down will undoubtedly be the airline industry. Oil provides 90% of our transportation energy and the cost of aviation fuel has more than doubled since the beginning of 2004. The profitability of airlines is coming under increasing pressure because of competition and soaring energy costs. Their other major headache, terrorism, has seen the cost of airport security soar.

On 20 January 2010, Japan Airlines announced it had filed for bankruptcy and laid off one third of its workforce with immediately effect, 15,600 jobs. This was one of Japan's biggest ever corporate failures but it's not the only national carrier in a tailspin. Also in deep trouble is US flagship American Airlines who have been forced to cut routes as a result of the high cost of aviation fuel. In the UK Ryanair and easyJet have only just managed to stay profitable by managing to fix or hedge the price that they pay for aviation fuel but eventually even this fixed rate price will expire. In 2012 Hungary's national airline Malev went bust as did Air Australia.

Within the next ten years, the rate of worldwide oil extraction will be unable to meet demand and the price of aviation fuel will rocket. Weaker airlines will go out of business and then the airline industry itself will collapse,

189

almost overnight. The last to go will be the big flag carriers from the Middle East, where most of the world's easily extracted oil is left. Emirates have recently ordered 45 new Airbus A380s; they can keep going for perhaps another 20 years but they may well be the last of the big commercial carriers.

At this juncture in time the Mayor of London, Boris Johnson in cahoots with the architect Lord Foster has unveiled a proposal to develop a £20 billion four-runway airport with twice the capacity of London Heathrow on a piece of land in the Thames estuary. Part of a wider integrated transport network that would link to high sped rail costing £50 billion. It seems like a political decision rather than one based on any kind of logic.

The need for high speed rail investment is not in doubt. As oil prices continue to rise, the world economy will be plunged into a deep depression with an accompanying increase in inflation and there will be massive disruption to air transportation. With a huge new airport as the "hub" of the nation's transport network the mayor is about to let his enthusiasm run away with his common sense leaving the UK with a £50 billion white elephant. By the middle of this century the air industry will have all but disappeared and those privileged few who can fly will either be rich or high-ranking government officials.

No matter how much we reduce our consumption of energy in the developed world, that's rich nations like America, Canada, France and Germany, there are still more and more people in developing nations like India, Brazil and China, who will take up the slack of energy consumption, driving us all on to shortage. Building schools, providing safe drinking water, producing food, all of this relies on oil. Renewables will never fill the fossil fuel gap. Even the energy required to build renewable energy sources like wind turbines rely on oil. In 2008 Jeroen van der Veer, Shell's chief executive, in an e-mail to his staff, let the cat out of the bag that output of conventional oil and gas was close to peaking. It said: "Shell estimates that after 2015 supplies of easy-to-access oil and gas will no longer keep up with demand." (1)

Since then the US military no less has come out and warned the world that there is likely to be serious oil shortages by 2015 and that these shortages will have a significant economic and political impact on us all. Without surplus oil we have no growth in our economies and without growth we rapidly go back to the dark ages with people killing each other for the last of the goodies in the supermarkets.

The impending energy crisis was detailed in a report from the US Joint Forces Command: "By 2012, surplus oil production capacity could entirely disappear, and as early as 2015 the shortfall in output could reach nearly 10 million barrels per day," says the report. It continues: "While it is difficult to predict precisely what economic, political, and strategic effects such a shortfall might produce, it surely would reduce the prospects for growth in both the developing and developed worlds. Such an economic slowdown would exacerbate other unresolved tensions, push fragile and failing states further down the path toward collapse, and perhaps have serious economic impact on both China and India." (2)

At the moment the world consumes 87 million barrels of oil per day. Professor Ian Fells, one of the world's most respected energy experts believes the world cannot produce more that 100 million barrels per day (see Q&A) and that point is rapidly approaching. Former BP chief Tony

Hayward told the BBC that the 100m bpd barrier would be crossed in 2020. (3)

Hayward's old job at BP came to an abrupt end after the Deepwater Horizon disaster of 2010. The very fact that BP needed to drill so far offshore is a clear indicator that there's no more big reserves of easily found oil to be found anywhere on dry land.

New Labour were advised of a world shortage of oil coming in 2015 but chose to ignore the warning: "The next major supply constraint, along with spiking oil prices, will not occur until recession-hit demand grows to the point that it removes the current excess oil stocks and the large spare capacity held by OPEC. However, once these are removed, possibly as early as 2012/2013 and no later than 2014/2015, oil prices are likely to spike, imperilling economic growth and causing economic dislocation." (4)

If you want to place a bet on the date of the next big oil spike then 2015 is the nearest thing you'll ever get to a dead cert, that's if the Straits of Hormuz haven't already become a battleground.

In 2008 a report was published, A Pragmatic Energy Policy for the UK. It was the work of Professor Ian Fells, an energy specialist who had advised successive British governments on energy policy.

It warned that the UK would experience prolonged power cuts by the middle of the next decade, that's around 2015. EU directives were forcing Britain to cut a third of its generation capacity.

The third in question was being generated by Britain's oil and coal-fired power stations which do not meet the EU requirement for carbon capture and storage. This carbon capture and storage is a system which operates nowhere in the world because it has not yet been invented! Such lunacy was exposed by Professor Fells who calculated that the closure of these power stations would result in an energy gap of 23 gigawatts (GW) of electricity generating capacity between now and 2020 with the widespread power shortages before then, in 2015.

The UK's nuclear reactors are to be decommissioned over the next decade leaving only one workable reactor by 2023. Professor Fells points out that we have signed up to an EU directive that binds us to having 20% of our energy made by renewables by 2020. Fells believes we will miss that target and the result will be the lights going out all over Britain.

According to the EU directive the UK was supposed to generate 10% of its energy from renewables by 2010. It managed to achieve six per cent but only because of taxpayer subsidies amounting to more than £1billion for renewable energy in 2007. That kind of money we no longer have, yet we must still abide by the directive.

I talked to Professor Fells at his home in Newcastle.

GC: Professor Fells, in your 2008 report A pragmatic Energy Policy for the UK you said that we faced power cuts in five years time, on that time scale that would be 2013 unless urgent action is taken. Do you still stand by that?

IF: Yes absolutely, and it's rather depressing that the situation hasn't changed very much. Using the Governments own figures they say that we lose through the next decade 23GW of electricity generating capacity, and that's about a third of our generating capacity and that consists mostly of old coal-fired stations which will not meet the new combustion plant emission standard from the

European Union, and nuclear stations which are just
coming to the end of their lives. I mean, a lot of the nuclear
stations are 40 years old. Calder Hall, the first one which is
being decommissioned is 50 years old. I mean, what is
amazing is that they've actually lasted but you can't go on
keeping them going. So we lose about a third of our
generating capacity and that has to be replaced. Now what is
going to replace it? The Government places great store by
renewable energy and in particular wind power which is
absurd because wind power doesn't really provide a secure
supply of electricity because it's intermittent.

In fact over the last, over Christmas and the New Year I
think there was an anticyclone over Western Europe and
wind power generated less, I think less than a half a per cent
of electricity, well less than one per cent of electricity right
across Europe and in the UK and because it was very cold
what kept everything going was coal-fired power stations.
So to think that you can rely on wind is a ludicrous thing to
do but the Government seems to think we'll build more
and more offshore wind farms and things like that. Well,
first of all you can't build them anything like as fast as they
would like to see them built. Secondly they are extremely
expensive and thirdly it's taken us, oh, 12 years to get
renewable energy from 3 per cent to 6 per cent, which is
what it is at the moment. But to get it to what they want
you'd have to multiply it about fivefold in a decade, which
is clearly not going to happen. So wind power is not going
to fill the gap.

GC: The 2007 Energy white paper called for the
building of more nuclear power stations. How many of
these will be producing power by the time the energy
crunch comes as you've suggested round about 2013?

IF: Well, the very optimistic predictions from Electricity De France is that they could have one up and running by 2018 but they haven't really got through all the planning procedures yet, they're still holding consultations. That would be Hinkley Point in Somerset. So I think to be realistic we might have two new nuclear power stations by 2020. Just two, and that would be two and a half GW. Now we're short of 23GW. The default situation is to build more gas-fired stations but even I can only find nine gas-fired plant which are in the pipeline. So that's really not going to solve the problem and the Government's sat on its hands and that's why we were predicting shortages by about 2014 and now, after criticism of me by the Government, now their chief scientist is predicting by about 2016 and Ofgem by about 2016, 2017. So its a pretty poor lookout but they've been warned about this for years and they've done nothing about it.

GC: So what can close the gap, can anything close the gap? It's an EU directive that we have to close down the polluting coal-fired power stations so what will happen when we haven't replaced the 23 GW of energy that we've lost?

IF: Well, I think what will happen is we'll just keep them going (coal-fired plants) I think we'll apply to the EU for what is called derogation. In other words please can we be let off this thing, which we may or may not get. But we'll have to keep the coal-fired stations going, you can't keep the nuclear stations going much longer and in desperation we'll have a rush job of building some gas fired stations....or the lights will go out which happened this year. Companies on interruptible gas-tariffs.... 100 companies were just cut off, that's manufacturing companies. The next to have been cut off would have been the gas-run power stations. Now that's a very serious matter,. It's no good saying oh we got over it all right. Not if you've had to close down a great chunk of your manufacturing industry to keep the lights on in the homes, and that's been rather glossed over.

GC: You did say we had better pray for a miracle come the middle of this decade. What do you think are the likely consequences of an Energy Crunch and how different would our society look with less energy or with having to ration energy?

IF: Well I remember the three day week back in 1974 very well when you only had electricity for three days in the week and you knew what times it was going to be switched on and that meant my kids had to do their homework by candle-light and companies just couldn't continue to run. People forget very quickly but they're not going to forget this time. Ofgem itself, which is the government, has predicted the price of electricity will go up by 60 per cent by 2015. Now that's horrifying, horrifying.

GC: I'm sure you know the views of M. King Hubbert who predicted that oil production worldwide would peak in 2005. Do you believe we've finally reached the stage where demand has finally outpaced production?

IF: Economists don't believe there's any limit to the oil that we can produce but then economists are very strange people and they think that the higher the price then the more oil appears but ultimately it is a finite resource. About 18 months ago I was at a big international meeting in Italy at which I was speaking where the consensus was that the world would probably not be able to produce more than 100 million barrels a day. At the moment I think we use 85 million barrels a day. And it was thought by many people there that 100 million barrels a day was maximum and that then it would decline by about two per cent a year, which is quite fast. People have argued a great deal about this since then and said what about all the other things coming on-stream like Tar Sands in Canada and so on...and that mollifies things a little bit but I suspect that this question of peak oil is a real factor and that should be taken into account anyway. We should be getting off the oil hook you know. It's like a drug really...particularly in America. I mean we wouldn't be having all this trouble drilling for oil if the American's didn't have an insatiable demand for it. (5)

Oil fuels growth in all modern economies and without growth we are unable to feed our huge surplus populations. The problem is now almost too big for us to solve. Global population grew by 140% between 1950 and 2000. World population is projected to top 9 billion in 2050, up from 6.8 billion this year and 7 billion early in 2012, the UN estimates.

According to the International Organization for Migration nearly all migrants from Africa are now living in Europe. Most travel from North Africa; from Algeria, Morocco and Tunisia. The Migration Policy Institute believes there are between seven and eight million irregular African immigrants living in the EU. That is, those who have entered Europe illegally or without documentation. An increasing number are travelling from sub-Saharan Africa; from Ghana, Nigeria, Somalia, Senegal and Turkey. Nearly all of them heading for western Europe; Holland, Norway, Sweden, Denmark and the UK.

If we had the time, the humanist solution would be to encourage the empowerment of women in the Third World. This would bring more jobs, better health services and lower levels of infant mortality and in developing nations would lead to lower birth rates and the adoption of sustainable growth.

The trouble is we haven't got the time, it may already be too late. The rate of population increase will win the race to the finish line of world starvation before we have a chance to stop it. Even before the 'perfect storm' of 2030 the developing world will be in a state of severe crisis, its starving peoples migrating north.

The world won't descend into barbarism over one weekend. There will be signs along the way, there may even be a short lived economic recovery in America and Europe but as this small recovery, maybe 18 months at best, eats up the last of OPEC's oil reserves prices will rise and rise.

Even if the West could count on the revolutionaries in North Africa and Iraq turning the oil taps back on at full pelt the $200 plus cost of a barrel of oil would dip back to maybe $100 for less than a year of the 18-month recovery blip before demand sends it soaring away again and we watch the world's big economies come crashing down. Another recession, this time longer, would be followed by a shorter recovery blip, this time less than a year before the next crash, and so on until the world economy flatlines permanently.

The billions of extra mouths we have to feed now are supplied by an agricultural process which turns oil into food. Oil is turned into fertiliser and pesticides to grow food and then used as fuel to transport it around the world. Food prices will begin to shoot up and the world's food supply will be reduced to a fraction of its current level. That's when those who cannot afford to pay will go without and millions in the earth's overpopulated regions will try to reach countries where there is still a plentiful supply, or die in the attempt. By 2030 most economists will admit "that's all folks" and its every man for himself. What happens then will not be pretty.

When it comes down to just how many people will be left alive after the effects of overpopulation coupled with huge energy shortages are taken into account the eminent scientist James Lovelock is unequivocal:

"When one tries to get at a number, my guess is somewhere between 500 million and 1 billion. No more than that. We will see in this century the most dreadful cull, and people will be driven either to the Arctic basin, which will be the last remaining tolerable climate where food can be grown, or to smaller oases on the continents in the mountainous areas. Ironically, the origins of our species, somewhere in the mountains of Kenya, may be the place where people go back in Africa, and are the last survivors. (6)

Thanks to New Labour's reckless immigration experiment we in Britain face the awful prospect of an overpopulated dystopia hobbled by energy shortages and growing unrest from resentful migrants and fearful trade unionists.

In 1998 when they had just gained power the government's own accounting service The Office for National Statistics (ONS) gave us its predictions based on current trends. They said that the population of Britain would increase at a slow rate to 65 million by 2051 and then decline slowly. That's what might have been.

Immigration at those levels would have been entirely manageable, we may well have remained a stable and prosperous nation in the short term despite the buffeting of the credit crunch. Only 10 years later (in 2008) the picture was very different. New Labour's open door immigration policies had changed that estimate dramatically.

ONS figures now stated that the UK population would rise to 77 million by 2051, that's another 12 million people and that by 2083 they expected the UK population to be 85 million. If there had been no mass immigration numbers would have settled at about 62 million by 2061.

That is now the future, and if multiculturalism can make any of us feel any safer or happier then there needs to be a sea change in efforts to integrate Britain's new parallel immigrant communities: hostile, resentful and now a feature of our British cities. Without a booming economy.... even with a booming economy, how are we to achieve all this? What kind of perverse liberal guilt is it that allowed politicians to transform our society without any consultation? What we are about to experience and what our children will be forced to live through is the loss of the welfare state that guaranteed safety to our stable population in tandem with large scale upheavals in the global economy.

Despite our island defences, we will be the worst prepared to weather what's now just around the corner.

"There is no living thing that is not afraid when it faces danger. The true courage is in facing danger when you are afraid."
  - L Frank Baum , The Wonderful Wizard of Oz.

Chapter Fourteen
What Is To Be Done?

New Labour had no interest in moderating the flow of immigration during the economic boom years of 1997 to 2004, when almost all of the unemployment among native Britons could have been mopped up with small changes to the welfare system. The requirement to take a job or lose benefits, incentives to take poor quality jobs by adding a bounty to the minimum wage and taking the lowest paid out of tax would have left the British isles as the best placed nation in Europe to face the economic consequences of financial meltdown and the coming energy crunch.

Instead what happened was mass migration from low wage economies all over the world to Britain's relatively high wage economy with the lure of a job being almost of equal importance with that of welfare tourism.

It became common knowledge across the continent of African, the slums of Mumbai, war torn Iraq and backward Pakistan that a much bigger prize was there for the taking. Free money, housing, health care, social care and education. All the riches of a fully-fledged welfare state unheard of in any developing economy and all you needed was a one way ticket to Sweden, Holland, Norway, Denmark or best of all, Britain.

The ruthless opening up of markets to low wage labour gave Britain something it had never experienced before, structural unemployment. From now on, even when the economy is temporarily growing, unemployment will always be with us.

Until the financial crash of 2008 leading globalists like Tony Blair and Gordon Brown were emphatic in their belief that ever increasing free trade, the free movement of labour and the internationalisation of financial markets would increase economic activity by making nations more interdependent thereby reducing the risk of conflict and war.

Forgotten, ignored or never understood in the first place was that the very peace and prosperity constant to Britain from 1945 to 1979 had been built on a broadly protectionist consensus of Labour and Conservative governments.

For the new globalists the first thing to do was strip Britain of all trade tariffs and embargos, especially those measures which protected jobs and prevented mass inward movement of labour from overseas.

The removal of tariff protection from steel making, coal mining, shipbuilding and the selling off of our power utilities to the highest bidders completed stage one. The next stage was to rigidly adhere to EU regulations allowing imports from low wage economies like China and India free access to Britain. That was a killer blow to jobs as mature economies like Britain's, paying much higher wages, could not compete.

Thus our higher priced quality goods were driven off the market while the new captains of globalised industry transferred our manufacturing capacity abroad to be operated by low wage labour.

By joining the EU we also became bound by treaties which insisted that there should be no protectionist borders in a free market and so further committed us to the other great folly of laissez-faire dogma, the free movement of people across borders.

That idea might have worked had there been an effective way of policing who came in and out of Europe, but successive waves of non-European immigrants soon found out that claiming asylum was a sure-fire way into Europe by the back door.

After New Labour signed up to the Human Rights Act in 1998 Britain became bound by the strictures of Article 3 prohibiting torture or inhumane treatment and a veritable stampede gathered pace. At first glance it seems fair enough that we cannot deport any person to a country where he or she would be at risk of "torture or inhumane treatment", even if that's where they came from. However, not only does this law now prevent the deportation of terrorists like Abu Qatada it also acts as an incentive for others like him to come to Britain, knowing they can never be returned to their countries of origin.

There are thousands of examples of how the application of the Human Rights Act has worked out in practice since

1998. The consequences of granting entry to many of those arriving in Britain illegally have been dire.

In 2001 Aso Ibrahim arrived in Britain from Iraq, smuggled on the back of a lorry. He applied for political asylum but was refused because he had suffered no persecution in Kurdish Iraq. Yet he was still allowed to remain in Britain. In 2003 and by now a disqualified driver he knocked down and killed a young girl, Amy Houston, then ran off. He was caught and sentenced to four months imprisonment. After his release he committed more driving offences as well as burglary and theft. When an attempt was made to deport him an English judge decided that this would breach his human rights which guaranteed him the right to a family life as he had since then fathered two young children by a British woman.

In another case from 2011 a Congolese asylum seeker William Danga violently raped and molested two young children, one aged just four years old, at the same time as he was fighting deportation on human rights grounds, using legal aid.

Danga, 39, had been convicted of raping a 16 year old girl in 2001 and sentenced to 10 years in jail; he was released in 2006. After being freed he remained in Britain courtesy of Article 8 of the Human Rights Act, guaranteeing him access to a family life in Britain as he had since fathered children by an 18-year-old English girl.

The girls who were six and four when they were raped were forced to give evidence in court against Danga, who screamed abuse at their relatives as he was led away to the cells. Whether Danga is deported on completion of his sentence is open to question.

In December 2011 the European Court of Justice said no-one should be returned to a country if it did not uphold their 'fundamental rights'.

More than 90 % of illegal immigrants who make their way to Europe do so through Greece and this ruling means that Britain cannot send asylum seekers back to Greece until its asylum system is working properly, which also means that anyone now wanting to enter Britain illegally has only to say they came here from Greece and they are granted automatic entry.

These and many more ECHR verdicts that defy any sense of natural justice or even common sense are alienating large sections of the British public who, historically, have always fought to overthrow bad justice.

Charles the First usurped the will of Parliament when misusing his personal rule through an unaccountable Court of Star Chamber to try cases of sedition, a kangaroo court that was used to kill off any opposition to his policies. These Star Chamber sessions were held in secret: there were no indictments, no right of appeal, no juries, and no witnesses. It became synonymous with the King's misuse of power during his Personal Rule. He was executed in 1688 by the will of Parliament and the people after being found guilty of treason. The passing of the English Bill of Rights Act 1689 brought to an end the concept of the divine right of kings. For the first time it made English kings and queens subject to laws passed by Parliament. This was the Glorious Revolution the English Civil War had been fought over. Parliament's legitimacy as the final power in the land has been in place ever since.

Until now, because now unelected judges are reviewing decisions made by the British Parliament and finding them to be unlawful. Parliament's legitimacy is again being usurped. Decisions dished out from European judges should be viewed as no more than guidance, so if Parliament decides not to give prisoners the vote, for instance, then that is the end of it. UN resolution 16/18 is about to test how attached we are to our right to freedom of speech.

Surely the rights of terrorists cannot be placed above the rights of ordinary citizens to be protected from terrorists? It seems not when it comes to men like Abu Qatada.

The cost to the UK of rulings and payouts due to the Human Rights Act have been so far been estimated at £42 billion, that's about half of the total cuts (£83 billion) outlined by George Osborne in his budget. The hope that the ECHR could become the default setting for civilised behaviour that could bring Islamic states to account is an expensive pipedream. Turning into a nightmare is its baleful influence as PC law steadily eats away at the moral fabric of British society.

In a report called Britain and the ECHR, author Dr Lee Rotherham concluded: "The cost of complying with judgements under the ECHR is £2.1 billion a year, with an additional £1.8 billion in one off costs", and went on to show that the cost in legal fees alone to the British taxpayer was some £17.3 billion.

Dr Rotherham believes that the European Convention on Human Rights (ECHR) "remains controversial as it forces changes in legislation that the British public and politicians do not want, such as allowing prisoners to vote."

The report concluded that the only way that problem would be solved was by withdrawing from the ECHR, or "the European Court changing its stance to respect a new British Bill of Rights." (1)

Islam calls for the removal of infidel invaders from their lands and on that they are correct in that the £12.6 billion a year we spend and the $105 billion a year America spends fighting for hearts and minds that can never be won in Afghanistan could be better spent elsewhere. (2)

We can no more create a liberal democratic state in Afghanistan than we could in Iraq or anywhere else in the Muslim world. The people of Libya, Tunisia and Egypt may have thrown off the chains of their oppressors but there is no doubt their new societies will still be faith based. Nor can we continue fooling ourselves that Muslim immigrants to Britain will ever want to assimilate into what they see as our decadent way of life.

Despite the lavish generosity of our welfare state towards the Muslim community and their obvious material enrichment it is clear that most of the Muslims who chose to come and live in Britain have little interest in adopting the values and customs of this country because no nation is as important to them as the supranational teachings of Islam.

Rational discrimination now makes it essential that if we are to preserve our values we must stop any more Muslim dependents permanent entry into Britain while at the same time encouraging those already here to assimilate. These measures would include the emancipation of Muslim women from the tyranny of their families, the restructuring of the welfare benefit system to encourage smaller family units and a ban on first cousin marriage.

As was the case in Denmark, until recently, no new citizens would be able to claim welfare benefits for a period of seven years after entry into Britain and any immigrants of dual citizenship committing a criminal offence after acquiring British citizenship would lose that citizenship and be deported without appeal on completion of their sentence as would those who would seek to replace our rule of law with Sharia law or by incitement to violence.

Britain is not a Muslim country and the British people have no desire for it to be transformed into one. In accordance with this there should be no more faith schools on British soil. The ones that remain must be rigorously monitored and prevented from encouraging hatred and violence towards Christians and Jews.

Ayyan Hirsi Ali, herself a Muslim, advised Britain on the immediate action necessary to stop the spread of radical Islam: "Close the Islamic faith schools today....Britain is sleepwalking into a society that could be ruled by sharia law within decades unless Islamic schools are shut down and young Muslims are instead made to integrate and accept western liberal values. We have to show the next generation of Muslims, the children, that they have a choice, and to do that — to have any hope whatsoever — we have to close down the Islamic faith schools." (3)

Muslim children must be encouraged to attend non-faith schools and in accord we need to ensure that the Muslim Council of Britain has no influence on our state education. Our freedoms are now threatened by Islamic nations using the UN as a means to disarm all criticism of Islamic practices. Britain cannot take any moral leadership within the confines of the ECHR and so must leave it in order for Parliament to regain its authority. Only then can we pass a British Bill of Rights that is not under the legal thumb of the ECHR and politicised European judges. Only then can Britain really stand up and once again take a world lead for freedom, democracy and equality. There must also be the equivalent of the American first amendment guaranteeing the right to free speech incorporated into a new British Bill of Rights, before it's too late.

The British people are increasingly scared of the implicit threat of violence posed by radical Islam and fear expressing these opinions in public in case they fall foul of the law. A recent poll showed that 69% of those surveyed believed we have too many immigrants in Britain. The sacrifice of our hard won liberties, made as a way of appeasing Islam, has not been worth it.

Those imams who feel they cannot commit to Britain until it has been transformed into a religious Islamic state will be allowed to leave. We are a tolerant people who have shown our Muslim guests generosity and friendship in the hope that this friendship will one day be reciprocated. Muslims can be assured that they can continue to live in Britain in peace and security; the Islamists who want Britain to be an Islamic state governed by Sharia law cannot. Therefore we need an immediate end to all immigration from fundamentalist Islamic nations like Pakistan while extending our welcome to multiethnic democracies like India.

The prevailing belief within the political elite that govern us in Britain is that if we continue to offer concessions to Islamists and give in to their demands they will become less demanding of us, that there is a majority of moderate Islamic opinion out there that can be reasoned with. The guiding belief of Islamists is not love thy neighbour but conquer him with no peace until the whole world is ruled by one huge Islamic state. Endless violence and war, jihad until the final victory. This basic information is not part of any media training course, perhaps it should be made available to print and broadcast journalists, especially those at the BBC, who were clearly effected by Arab spring "euphoria".

This struggle for supremacy has been Islam's motivating force for 1400 years and if it were possible to pursue jihad by open warfare in the West this would be the policy of the Islamists. This is why Iran is striving to build an atomic bomb. When Iran says it wants to wipe Israel off the face of the Earth, believe it. They haven't got the technology at the moment but in the meantime Islam hopes to conquer Europe by out-breeding its native population. Opposing this "jihad by stealth" will require courage and the willingness of patriotic individuals to stand up and be counted.

What we need is concrete evidence that democracy is compatible with Islamic thinking. Without it there must be no leniency from our judiciary for those who call for jihad and seek to impose Islamic rule or promote suicide terrorism, second class citizenship for non-Muslims, the death penalty for adultery or apostasy and honour killings of women. This conduct has no place in any civilised society and those who advocate it must be stripped of their citizenship and removed from British soil. This cannot be achieved within the strictures of the ECHR so we must withdraw from that agreement as soon as is possible.

National Review columnist and director of the Middle East Forum, Daniel Pipes wrote: "Muslims are entitled to equal rights and responsibilities but not to special privileges. They must fit into the existing order, not remake Western societies in the Islamist mould. Increasing freedom is welcome, regressing to the medieval norms of the Sharia is not." (3)

There is no reason why the Koran cannot be reinterpreted and reformed by enlightened Islamic scholars if they are free from the threat of intolerance and violence. Without reform we will see political Islam gain more and more leverage over our fragile and hard won freedoms.

Winston Churchill first began to warn of the dangers of fascist Germany against all prevailing opinion, and his was a lone voice. He was effectively banned from BBC airwaves before World War Two after being labelled an extremist for railing against the stated intentions of Hitler and the Nazis. Churchill had made a detailed study of Mein Kampf and had bullet-pointed Hitler's aims. Comparing it to the Koran he said:

"All was there - the programme of German resurrection, the technique of party propaganda; the plan for combating Marxism; the concept of a National Socialist state; the rightful position of Germany at the summit of the world. Here was the new Koran of faith and war: turgid, verbose shapeless, but pregnant with its message." (4)

These are huge undertakings and it may already be too late, but we must make the effort before we sleepwalk into a nightmare world deprived of rationality, tolerance and freedom.

END

Appendix 1
M. King. Hubbert

The man known as King Hubbert was born in Texas in 1903. He gained a PhD in geology and physics in 1937 at the University of Chicago and then taught geophysics at Columbia University until 1941 before becoming a research geophysicist with the Shell Oil Company.

In 1948, Hubbert predicted that for any given geographical area the rate of petroleum production over time would resemble a bell curve. This became known as the Hubbert Curve. His prediction that US oil production would peak in 1970 proved to be correct. In 1974, Hubbert stated that 'if current trends continue' global oil production would peak in 1995.

After the effects of the OPEC oil embargo of 1973 were extrapolated he modified this prediction to say that the effect of this embargo would delay the peak by a decade. That makes the date of worldwide peak production 2005, a date most experts within the oil industry now quietly accept as fact.

Appendix 2
Zero Per Cent Freedom

D r Peter Hammond in his book Slavery Terrorism and
Islam: The Historical Roots and Contemporary
Threat looked at the way Islamists are able to first establish
themselves in liberal western society then agitate for change
using threats of violence and the manipulation of the
tolerant and politically correct. As the percentage of
Muslims grow in each country so do their demands. For the
purposes of an accurate comparison I have updated Dr
Hammonds statistics to 2011 with statistics provided by the
non-partisan Pew Research group. The underlined quotes
come from Dr Hammond.

**As long as the Muslim population remains around
of under 2% in any given country, they will be for the
most part regarded as a peace loving minority, and
not as a threat to other citizens.**

Country	Muslim 2011	Muslim 2030
USA	0.8	1.7
Australia	1.9	2.8

| China | 1.8 | 2.1 |

At 2% to 5% they begin to proselytize from other ethnic minorities and disaffected groups, often with major recruiting from the jails and among street gangs.

Canada	2.8	6.6
Italy	2.6	5.4
Norway	3.0	5.4
Denmark	4.1	5.6
United Kingdom	4.6	8.2
Sweden	4.9	9.9
Spain	4.9	9.9

From 5% on they exercise an inordinate influence in proportion to their percentage of the population. For example, they will push for the introduction of halal (clean by Islamic standards) food, thereby securing food preparation jobs for Muslims. They will increase pressure on supermarket chains to feature halal on their shelves – along with threats for failure to comply. At this point they will work to get the ruling government to allow them to rule themselves (within their ghettos) under sharia, the Islamic law. The ultimate goal of Islamists is to establish sharia law over the entire world.

Germany	5.0	7.1
Holland	5.5	7.8
Switzerland	5.7	8.1
France	7.5	10.3

When Muslims approach 10% of the population they tend to increase lawlessness as a means of complaint about their conditions. In Paris, we are already seeing car burnings. Any non Muslim action offends Islam, and results in uprisings and threats, such as in Amsterdam, with opposition to Mohammed cartoons and films about Islam. Such tensions are seen daily, particularly in Muslim sections.

Russia	11.7	14.4
India	14.6	15.9
Israel	17.7	23.2

At 40% nations experience widespread massacres, chronic terror attacks, and ongoing militia warfare.

Lebanon	59.7	59.7

From 60% nations experience unfettered persecution of non-believers of all other religions (including non-conforming Muslims), sporadic ethnic cleansing (genocide), use of sharia law as a weapon, and jizyah, the tax placed on infidels.

Sudan	71.4	71.4
Qatar	77.5	77.5

After 80% expect daily intimidation and violent jihad, some state-run ethnic cleansing and even some genocide as these nations drive out the infidels and move toward 100% Muslim.

Albania	82.3	83.2
Indonesia	88.1	88.0

Bangladesh	90.4	92.3
Syria	92.8	92.8
Egypt	94.7	94.7
Iran	98	98
Iraq	98.9	98.9
Pakistan	96.4	96.4
Turkey	98.6	98.6
Tunisia	99.8	99.8
Morocco	99.9	99.9
Afghanistan	99.8	99.8
Saudi Arabia	97.1	97.1
Somalia	98.6	98.6
Yemen	99	99

100% will usher in the peace of 'Dar-es-Salaam' – the Islamic house of peace. At this stage there is supposed to be peace because everyone is a Muslim, the madrassas are the only schools and the Koran is the only word.

Muslims are set to become the majority of the world's population by the end of the century.

Appendix 3
America

March 15, 2012. President Obama leaned back on his upholstered leather chair in the Oval Office and sighed. It was all starting to get away from him. "Goddamn Dubya," he said quietly to himself. What a legacy, a 15 trillion dollar deficit now running away from him at the rate of $4 billion a day, the economy still in recession and worst of all, the Pakistan situation. On his desk the latest briefing from General Jones calling for a full scale invasion. This was now the consensus of the joint chiefs of staff and already leaked to the press, manna from heaven for the nutcon activists who believed a stand up knock-down reckoning with the Islamist controlled army over there was now the preferred option.

Obama reflected on his last head to head with General McChrystal who had leaned over the presidential desk in front of him and then threateningly intoned: "Mr President, after more than a trillion dollars spent and two thousand US servicemen dead we may as well have invaded Pakistan in the first place because that's where all the goddam terrorists came from, not Afghanistan."

The President knew that this was an accurate assessment and reviewed his options, admittedly none of them very appealing. Pakistan had received more than a billion dollars a year every year since 9/11 in order to neutralise Islamic terrorism and what had the US to show for all the money? The brass were upping the war ante after intelligence revealed the extent of Pakistan's surrender to the Taliban.

Yet he dared not sack another general for fear of provoking a constitutional crisis that was only averted after the death of Bin Laden. The escalation of the drone attacks in the Taliban held Pakistan border in 2011 had brought the people out onto the streets of Islamabad in their thousands.

The Pakistan Army, now directed by the ISI, had from the very beginning been using the billions of dollars successive American administrations had handed over to them not to help eradicate the Taliban but to ensure they were not defeated. A dangerous game of double dealing that had led to hardline Islamists infiltrating and then taking over the ISI, Pakistan's secret service. Taking the Yankee dollar with one paw while arming and advising the Taliban was an act of military schizophrenia the Pakistani government would come to regret. There had been had a huge surge in support for militant Islam in Pakistan who were now within an ace of their greatest triumph, the seizure and control of Pakistan's arsenal of around 50 missile-launched nuclear weapons.

"Mr President, we must do something now," General Petraeus had urged him, "according to our intelligence the Taliban will have complete control of Pakistan offensive nuclear capability within weeks, we cannot wait any longer, sir."

Not only did he have the generals baying for blood, there was also the Indian Premier who had said that should the military government in Pakistan fall he would be taking pre-emptive action to secure Kashmir neutrality. Should the Indian ultimatum he was preparing to deliver to Islamabad be ignored that city would be targeted for massive destruction.

Obama looked down at another report lying on his desk. This one commissioned by the US Academy of Sciences. This was the result of a study to determine the effects of an all-out nuclear war between India and Pakistan. Its authors, University of Colorado scientists Mills and Toon had used computer modelling to show that such a war would involve the use of approximately 100 Hiroshima sized atom bombs. "A little old-fashioned nuclear war", as one General had called it. Obama grinned ruefully to himself as an image from Kubrick's film Dr Strangelove involuntarily popped into his head. The bad news was that these small atom bombs would still blast five million tonnes of soot 80 km into the air absorbing enough solar radiation to set in motion a series of chemical reactions that would break down the stratospheric ozone layer protecting the earth from harmful ultraviolet radiation.

"We would see a dramatic drop in ozone levels that would persist for many years.... the ozone decrease would be up to 40 per cent, which could have huge effects on human and on terrestrial, aquatic and marine ecosystems." the report concluded.

The president then glanced at the National Resources Defence Council document that had kept him out of his bed last night. Their experts had been thinking the unthinkable. Using the most advanced computer simulations available they had come up with a likely scenario for a war between India and Pakistan, two nations that hated each other with a venom beyond the cold war bluster of America and the USSR. This was pure religious dogma, Hindu nationalism ranged against Islamic fundamentalism, and this time the mad mullahs had their finger on Pakistan's nuclear trigger and weren't going to blink while paradise awaited them.

"What's the worst-case scenario on this Bob?" Obama asked Robert Gates, his national security overlord. Gates cleared his throat and looked round at the graven faces surrounding the president.

"Well sir, what both sides have is the type of fission weapons we dropped on Hiroshima in '45, that was a 15 kiloton bomb but theirs may be slightly bigger, up to 25 kilotons."

"How many of these are going to actually blow up?" asked Obama.

"Pakistan has 48 warheads," continued Gates, "mounted on missiles and India has 35 bombs deployed on fighter aircraft. Given the primitive nature of Pakistan's missile guidance systems we estimate no more than 75 per cent target accuracy... around 95 for India."

"And what about casualties?"

"Because of the high urban densities of the targets each bomb would kill about four times as many people than the one dropped on Hiroshima. Our intelligence shows three warheads locked in on Bombay would result in 5 million blast deaths, three warheads on Delhi, 5 million dead, 3 warheads on Karachi ...5 million dead ..2 warheads on Lahore 5 million dead ..."

"What are we talking about in total casualties from both sides, Bob?", interrupted an increasingly agitated Obama.

"Probably 20 million dead initially with another 30 million affected by the fallout from the attacks, 50 million dead, that's a conservative estimate Mr President as we don't have the analysis of what the damage to the ozone would do to the mid-latitudes."

"Yes", thought Obama, ruefully "Armageddon time".

Appendix 3
How Much?

Nobel prize-winning economist Joseph Stiglitz estimated that the cost of war in Iraq came to more than \$3 trillion. Borrowed money that would wreck the American economy in years to come. Latest figures from the Congressional research service (CRS) show the US military spending \$2 billion a week in Afghanistan. That eclipses a much more conservative estimate released by the Pentagon in February 2010 showing a month by month spend of \$6.7 billion compared to \$5.5 billion in Iraq. That's \$8 billion a month on a war no-one outside the military thinks it can win. Come the drawdown and exit in 2014 a lot of American taxpayers will be wanting to know what they got for their money.

To put this into some kind of perspective, eight month's worth of this spending would have financed the entire Constellation Space Programme, cancelled by President Obama due to budgetary cutbacks. That peaceful endeavour could have transformed the global economy by creating thousands of new jobs and \$billions worth of technological by-products in the process of establishing a permanent human presence on the moon. It has now been cancelled, consigned to the page of wrong turns in US history along with the Civil War, the assassination of Abraham Lincoln and Bobby Kennedy and the Wall Street swindle of 2008.

With the killing of Osama Bin Laden the US has revealed a much bigger problem. He wasn't found in some remote cave, he was living in a walled town house 35 miles from the capital of Islamabad. In Abbotabad, where the Pakistani military has a strong presence and right next door to the Kakul military academy where most of its intelligence officers graduated.

The military men who run Pakistani were protecting Bin Laden because Pakistan has a vested interest in keeping Afghanistan a Muslim client state and a hostile buffer zone between it and its real enemy, India. As a consequence much civil society in Pakistan has become hostage to radical Islam leaving the US to worry about what to do when Pakistan becomes a militarised Islamist state with an armoury of nuclear weapons at the disposal of its new rulers.

America's slide towards economic depression and isolationism will continue after the departure of Barak Obama.

It was reported in 2011 that perfectly habitable three bedroomed houses are available to buy in Detroit for as little as $10,000, that's less than the cost of second-hand car, but that there is no demand even at that price. In the absence of a strong economic recovery the US housing market could be obliterated in the next two years as higher interest rates kick in on many loans. Even if there is growth this will only postpone the inevitable. The external national debt of the US was $15 trillion as of June 2009. What is of greater concern to the US Treasury is the mountain of concealed toxic assets (securities backed by dodgy mortgages) still on the books of major banks. The biggest shock is that the nation with the world's second biggest external debt, bigger than Japan, Greece Italy and Ireland's combined, is Britain.

Glossary

AD - Anno Domini.

AKP – Justice and Development Party (Turkey).

BNP – British National Party.

Carrying capacity – the number of people able to be sustained within the limits of natural resources.

ECB – European Central Bank

EDL – English Defence League.

EIA – Energy Information Administration.

EU - European Union.

HPA – Health Protection Agency.

IEA – International Energy Agency.

IMF – International Monetary Fund.

IPCC - Intergovernmental Panel on Climate Change.

MAC - Migration Advisory Council

MCB – Muslim Council of Britain.

ONS – Office for National Statistics.

OPEC – Organization of Petroleum Exporting Countries.

OPT - Optimum Population Trust.

PC – politically correct.

Q & A – Question and Answer.

UN - United Nations.

Bibliography

Chapter One: Space not Race

(1) ONS Migration Statistics Quarterly Report No8 Feb 2011.

(2) Rod Liddle, The Sunday Times Magazine, 10/4/2011

Chapter Two: Hideously White

(1) Maurice Glasman, Progress, May 2011.

(2) London Evening Standard 23/10/2009

(3) Royal Commission on the Conditions of the Poorer Classes in Ireland, Appendix G, The State of the Irish Poor in Great Britain, Parliamentary Papers (1836), XXXIV p. iii.

(4) The Road to Serfdom, F.A. Hayak, p222.

Chapter Three: The Road to 2020

(1) ONS updated 27/3/2011

(2) Marin Ivens, The Sunday Times, 4/12/11

(3) The Daily Mail, 16/12/09

(4) BBC London News 4/8/08

Chapter Four: Beyond the Fix

(1) Progress op cit.

(2) The Net National Costs of Immigration: Fiscal Effects of Welfare Restorations to Legal Immigrants, Donald Huddle, Rice University, 1997.

(3) Economic Affairs Committee of the House of Lords in 2007/08. First Report, 1 April, 2008.

(4) MigrationWatchUK, Immigration and Pensions study (1.24) 25/1/2010.

(5) www.migrationwatchuk 2/5/06

(6) The Daily Telegraph 24/2/11

Chapter Five: We'll Have To Go On Paying

(1) MigrationWatchUK briefing paper 11.32

(2) Sunday Times 20/3/11.

(3) Management of Asylum Applications by the UK Border Agency. 23.1.2009. ISBN 9781012954524.

(4) The Observer 27/2/2011.

(5) Frank Field, Cross Party Group on Balanced Migration 2008.

(6) Sunday Times May 3, 2009.

Chapter Six: Police and Thieves

(1) BBC Radio 5 live debate: England riots, three months on 14/11/11

Chapter Seven: Our Health and Safety

(1) The Guardian, 11/4/11

(2) The Daily Telegraph, 15/6/03

(3) The Daily Mail 11/5/2010

(4) Access to the NHS. Health 5.3. Consultation on NHS Primary Medical Services: MigrationWatch UK.

(5) The Daily Mail, 24/10/11

(6) The Times of India, Ban UK Pakistanis from marrying cousins, 17/11/2005

(7) Nicolai Sennels: Muslim Inbreeding: Impacts on intelligence, sanity, Health and Society, EuropeNews, 9/8/2010.

(8) Rockwool Foundation Research Unit, May 2007: Ethnic students does not make Danish children worse.

(9) Proceedings of the National Academy of Science, 1978, Effect of inbreeding on IQ and mental retardation.

(10) The Telegraph 24/12/2008.

(11) The Independent, 24/12/2008

(12) Jonathan Wynne-Jones Sunday Telegraph 3/2/2008.

(13) The Daily Telegraph, 21/3/11

(14) Nicholas Watt, The Guardian, 16/5/11

(15) It's Already Happened, James Meek, London Review of Books (Sept 2011)

Chapter Eight: Cities in Flight

(1) Wrong from Head to Toe: A ridiculous and ominous decision in Britain. Theodore Dalrymple, National Review March 28, 2005.

(2) Mailonline 16/12/2003.

(3) Op Cit.

(4) The Daily Mail 9/2/2010

(5) The Sikh Times 14/1/2003.

(6) The Daily Telegraph 5/2/11

(7) BBC News online 6/5/04

(8) The Guardian 4/5/04

(9) Ed Morrissey, Campus Watch, 19/11/08

(10) The Daily Telegraph 19/2/06

(11) The Daily Mail 23/9/10

(12) Cruel and Unusual Punishment: The Terrifying Global Implications of Sharia Law by Nonie Dawish (Thomas Nelson 2009)

(13) The Australian 20/9/10

(14) Broadcast on Al Jazeera 30/1/09

(15) melaniephillips.com 18/1/05

(16) Op.Cit. 18/1/05

Chapter nine: Dangerous Minds

(1) Channel Four, Dispatches, Lessons in Hate and Violence. 14/2/2011.

(2) Miranda Bryant, London Evening Standard, 18/1/2010.

(3)The Sun, 8/3/2011.

(4) The Daily Mail 27/2/12

(5) Channel Four, Dispatches, Undercover Mosque, 1/9/2008.

(6) Ian Traynor, The Guardian, 22/10 2010.

(7) Christopher Hitchens, Holland's shameful treatment of Ayaan Hirsi Ali. Slate, 3/2/2010.

(8)The Daily Telegraph,11/12/2004.

Chapter Ten: Europe on its Knees

(1) Karl Ritter, Associated Press 20/9/10

(2) The Daily Mail 12/11/10

(3) American Thinker 28/7/11

(4) The Daily Telegraph 3/1/11

(5) The Guardian 6/6/10

(6) Op. Cit. 6/6/10

(7) The Economist 17/7/08

(8) Op. Cit. 17/7/08

Chapter Eleven: Money-go-Round

(1) Interview in Focus magazine, 7/5/011.

Chapter Twelve: Population/Aid Growth

(1) The Daily Mail 11/5/11

(2) The Guardian 18/3/09

(3) The Daily Mail 10/6/11

(4) The Guardian 14/7/11

(5) The Oxford Times 19/2/09

Chapter Thirteen: The Energy Crunch of 2015

(1) The Times 25/1/2008.

(2) Terry Macalister guardian.co.uk 11/4/2010.

(3) BBC Radio 4, Feb 4, 2010.

(4) Second Report of the UK Industry Taskforce on peak Oil and Energy Security. February 2010.

(5) Professor Ian Fells. Interview with G.M.Cooke, Tuesday, July 6, 2010.

(6) James Lovelock, The Revenge of Gaia (2006) p133.

Chapter Fourteen: What Is To Be Done?

(1) Dr Lee Rotherham, Britain and the EHCR, Taxpayers Alliance Report, Dec 2010.

(2) The Guardian 13/2/09

(3) David Cohen, Evening Standard, 2/2/ 2007.

(4) danielpipes.org Two Decades of Rushdie Rules, October 2010.

(5) The Gathering Storm by Winston Churchill (London:Cassell 1948) p43.

Further Reading

Peter Hammond, Slavery, Terrorism and Islam: The Historical Roots and Contemporary Threat, (Xulon Press 2010).

Michael Lewis, The Big Short, (Large Print Press, 2011).

Lester Brown, Who Will Feed China? Wake -up Call For a Small Planet. (WW Norton, 1995).

Kenneth S. Deffeyes, Hubbert's Peak: The Impending World Oil Shortage, (Princeton University Press, 2001).

James Lovelock, Gaia: A New Look at Life on Earth, (Oxford University Press 1979).

Richard Heinberg, The Party's Over: Oil, War and the Fate of Industrial Societies, (Clairview 2003).

Richard Heinberg, Peak Everything, (Clairview 2006).

Dissent and Development: Studies and Debates in Development Economics by Peter Bauer (Harvard University Press 1972)

The Plot Against The NHS, Colin Leys and Stewart Player (Merlin Press 2001).

Bell Curve: Intelligence and Class Structure in American Life by Richard Herrnstein and Charles Murray (A Free Press Paperback 1996)

The Caged Virgin by Ayaan Hirsi Ali.

Islam: Past, Present and Future by Professor Hans Kung.

A Culture of Corruption: Everyday Deception and Popular Discontent in Nigeria by Daniel Jordan Smith

Dead Aid: Why Aid is not Working and How There is a Better Way for Africa by Dambisa Moyo

Printed in Great Britain
by Amazon.co.uk, Ltd.,
Marston Gate.